EVERGREEN

Annie Bell began her cookery career with a hands-on spell in the kitchen, firstly by setting up the small café at the back of the specialist bookshop Books for Cooks, and subsequently working as a chef. Children changed all that, and she now writes full-time. She writes on food and cookery for the *Independent* and has been cookery writer on *Vogue* since 1992. She continues to specialise in vegetarian cookery and is one of the principal exponents in the UK of the 'new wave' style that gained such recognition in California.

D1313459

Also by Annie Bell

A Feast of Flavours: The New Vegetarian Cuisine

EVERGREEN

Classic Vegetarian Cookery

ANNIE BELL

MACMILLAN

First published 1994 by Bantam Press

This edition published 1996 by Macmillan Reference Books
a division of Macmillan Publishers Limited
25 Eccleston Place, London SW1W 9NF
and Basingstoke

Associated companies throughout the world

ISBN 0-333-66068-4

1 3 5 7 9 8 6 4 2

A CIP catalogue record for this book is available from the British Library

Printed by Mackays of Chatham PLC, Chatham, Kent

To the memory of my brother Jamie Pike,
who died tragically in March 1992, with all my love.

Acknowledgements

My thanks go to Rosemary Sandberg, my agent, and Georgina Morley, my editor at Bantam Press, for their abiding support and encouragement. Thanks also to everyone at Bantam Press involved in producing the book; and to Books for Cooks, which remains a bastion for research and information; and to Clarissa Dickson-Wright.

On the home front, thanks to those who play 'mother' while I work, and of course to my husband, who tastes, reads, criticizes and praises duly, but always fairly. It would be impossible to mention my myriad sources of inspiration involved in putting a collection of recipes together: books, restaurants, meals in friends' homes, shops – I gather and garner.

Lastly my thanks to *Vogue* for allowing material first published in *Vogue* to be reproduced here, and to Georgina Boosey for her support.

Contents

Chilled and Hot Soups

Salads and Mezze

Eggs and Cheese

Mushrooms

Pizza, Calzone and Sandwiches

Pulses, Beans and Grains

Tarts and Pies

Hot and Cold Vegetable Dishes

Potatoes and Gnocchi

Pasta and Noodles

Rice and Polenta

Chocolate, Fruit Tarts and Other Puddings

Introduction

A thick, chilled gazpacho, vibrant and red with tomatoes, eaten with warm, fresh white bread, dipped first into olive oil and then into the soup. Or a Thai salad with thin strips of cucumber, char-grilled baby corn and aubergine, hot and sharp with chilli, lemon juice and sesame. A cheese soufflé risen inches above the rim of the dish into a glossy flat surface, crusty on the outside and ethereal and light inside. Button mushrooms infused with the aromatic flavours of a broth, with freshly chopped herbs and diced tomato stirred into them at the last minute. A thin pastry case spread with a sweet purée of onions, and sliced potatoes, covered with crème fraîche piquant with the flavour of finely grated fresh horseradish: I find vegetarian food fresh and sensual, and alive. Interesting and packed with textures and flavours, it is for me a complete celebration in eating. But there is no reason why as a vegetarian you should not also maintain a taste for *'petits pots au chocolat'*, made with a silky couverture chocolate, or an almond crumble baked over a base of raspberries and Cape gooseberries, smothered with a foamy kirsch sabayon. Likewise crème brûlée with a thin, crisp surface of caramel, and sticky toffee pudding studded with raisins soaked in sweet wine, then drowned in cream.

Becoming a vegetarian is often seen as a move towards a healthier diet, or equated with abstinence. The decision may be linked to moral, religious or political reasons. All these are relevant, but it is important not to confuse issues with food itself. A vegetarian diet can, like any other, range from the inedible to the sublime. Too often the vegetarian pie you buy is also labelled 'healthy pie' or 'cruelty-free pie' with no emphasis on its gastronomic value. I believe that the confusion of food with issues is an unfortunate one. It seems to haunt vegetarian food in a way in which no other cuisine is affected. Being a vegetarian should not automatically mean a denial of pleasurable foods, or an acceptance of unpalatable ones. A campaigner will put recipes in a book to encourage people, and in the past this has backfired miserably, damaging the reputation of vegetarian food in a way it does not deserve.

According to the Weasel, the *Independent Magazine*'s diary

columnist, 'Thousands of years of human experience have taught us that only a limited number of different foods and combinations of food are actually any good. Every now and then someone will invent a new dish that catches on, like crème brûlée, but the cook's main job is to seek to perfect the traditional dishes which everybody knows and likes.' The same premise forms the basis for this book. Familiarity often makes people return again and again to the same dishes, dishes which become a custom and are handed down from one person to another, so becoming traditions. But there is a pitfall: sometimes we are content to eat terrible versions of familiar dishes, allowing the comfort found in familiarity to override gastronomic good judgement. In this book I have drawn from as many different cuisines as possible. Every cuisine has some vegetarian traditions, some more than others. I have returned hungry from a weekend in Paris, almost starving after a week in St Petersburg, and in a blissful state, fit to burst, after a stay in Italy. Some dishes have simply received a quick buff, others a more radical rethink. But I have not forced newness on old favourites for the sake of it; perhaps a new twist here and there, some added detail and a touch of artistic licence.

In creating the recipes I have avoided frills and, in that sense, regard them as relatively simple. This does not mean they are always quick and easy to prepare, because the recipes rely on fresh ingredients and these do have to be prepared. My main concern has been to maximize the potential of each dish, which might involve skinning and deseeding 2 lb of tomatoes rather than opening a tin, or perhaps stripping corn kernels from the cob rather than turning to the Jolly Green Giant. Unfortunately most foods which come out of a tin taste of the tin. But other conveniences are very welcome: fresh shop-bought pasta, or passata in a jar, fresh vegetable stocks and so forth, are all fully exploited. I like to believe that any additional time spent in the preparation will be reflected in the quality of the finished dish.

I have tried to mix the quick and easy with the sophisticated. I did not specifically have entertaining in mind as I wrote the book, but would hope you would be as happy to serve these dishes at a party as at a simple supper. Many of the dishes are interchangeable as first or as main courses, and most of the recipes feed four, though the tarts will feed six. You will probably be able to judge from the quantity of ingredients how much you are making.

I have always taken immense pleasure in the process of cooking, almost as much as in the finished product. I love the way a recipe progresses and enjoy the chopping, the pounding, the stirring and rolling; I am happily lost in the process. Avoid rushing things; instead coax the best from your raw materials. Also, react to what you are cooking rather than following the text by the letter, because cooking is a living process and a recipe is there for guidance rather than as a rulesheet. In fact there are very few rules in cookery; what counts is intuition. I have tried to give as much detail as I feel is relevant. It is myth that a recipe which occupies five lines rather than ten is in fact quicker; quite possibly it means there is inadequate detail.

Both old and new classics are represented. Recent years have seen a number of dishes creeping on to menus or into shops in Britain which are part of food as we know it today, contemporary classics if you like. Some would argue that the very nature of traditional British food has been to borrow from abroad, so the trend towards an eclectic internationalism is only continuing the pattern of the past.

While vegetarians still account for only a small percentage of the population, a much higher percentage of people have cut down on meat and are eating more vegetarian food. This book is for anyone who eats just one vegetarian meal a week through to those who are strictly committed. It is founded on my personal love for a way of eating which offers some of the best possible gastronomic experiences.

TERMS

My time spent as a chef has left a mild hangover of culinary terms which might not be familiar to every reader. These are few rather than many, but occasionally it is easier to give the professional designation for a particular process, and it saves on repetitive lengthy explanations. The following are terms I feel to be of some use.

Chiffonade: To prepare a chiffonade of sorrel or basil, place several leaves on top of each other, roll them into a tight scroll and cut across the scroll to give thin strips of the leaf.

Concassée: *Concasser* is French for chopping or pounding. Tomato concassée is the skinned and seeded flesh of tomatoes, finely diced.

Julienne: This is food cut into thin squared strips. First the food is thinly sliced (a mandolin will assist here), then the slices are cut into thin strips 1-2 inches/2-5cm long.

SPECIFICATIONS

Arachide Oil

Also called groundnut or peanut oil, this is neutral-tasting and suitable for deep-frying or for use in combination with stronger oils.

Butter

Use an unsalted butter. The Normandy 'd'Insigny' butter is very good.

Chillies

In Mexico and much of the United States chillies are chipotle, jalapeño, serrano and ancho. In Britain chillies are just chillies, and the varieties found for sale are rarely labelled with their type. There are hundreds of varieties of chilli; an oily substance, capsaicin, is responsible for their fiery, spicy quality, and while a jalapeño chilli can contain 2,500 to 3,000 Scoville units, a measurement of its heat, the habañero can have up to 300,000. This makes specifying quantities for recipes difficult. The sophistication of cooking with chillies is fully explored in Elizabeth Lambert Ortiz's wonderful *Encyclopedia of Herbs, Spices and Flavourings*, which is one of the most useful books any cook can have. I have erred on the side of caution in the following recipes by suggesting quite conservative quantities, and I have always used the long thin chillies generally found in a supermarket, Serrano chillies.

Green chillies are unripe, and red are ripe. Prepare chillies with care, avoiding contact with the skin, and especially the face and eyes. Both the seeds and the ribs contain capsaicin and are generally removed before use, as is the skin. But for the small quantities called for in the following recipes I just chop them finely without removing the skin.

Eggs

The size of egg is specified in each recipe. Store them at room temperature, the fresher the better.

Goat's Cheeses

These vary in maturity from being very fresh (the unsalted ones are more like a yoghurt) through to mature ones of overwhelming pungency. All the recipes which follow call for a medium-mature or demi-sec cheese, although certain small mature cheeses can also bake well. Crottin de Chavignol is perhaps the best known of the French cheeses, and there is an excellent Spanish equivalent preserved in olive oil with herbs. There are also some good British imitations, especially the Innes cheeses. To date I have not found a suitable cheese in a supermarket, although occasionally in desperation I turn to the slices of *'chèvre'*, but this is too assertive to be ideal.

Olive Oil

If a recipe specifies olive oil rather than extra virgin olive oil, it means that either a pure or an extra virgin olive oil can be used and the quality is not too important. If the recipe specifies extra virgin olive oil, you should use a cheaper commercially produced oil to cook with, and save the good estate-bottled oils for salads or for use in their raw state where their quality will be appreciated. Once you heat an oil it completely alters, most of the original flavour is lost.

Pepper

Unless the recipe states otherwise, pepper means freshly ground black peppercorns: hot and aromatic. Some recipes call for freshly ground white pepper, which is less spicy and better suited to white sauces or very delicate dishes, or cayenne where the desired effect is a hot and piquant punch.

Salt

Use sea salt, either fine grain or a coarse grain in a grinder. Until a recent trip to Sicily I believed that sea salt was sea salt: then I discovered Trapani sea salt. A visit to the salt pens on the shore of this town on the Southern coast changed my conception. These salt flats were a thriving industry in Sicily during the last century – windmills provided power as seawater passed into successive tanks, the concentration of salt in the water increasing in each one. Eventually the water becomes saturated with salt and it settles out from the water. At this final stage it is mounded into white crystalline piles, a sight to be seen from the surrounding hills on a moonlit night. This is an unrefined salt, retaining many of the sea's minerals, and when it is sprinkled over food it does have a flavour of the sea, and it is sweeter and less aggressive than the sea salt more widely available. There are a handful of enlightened shops where you might find it; in fact most of the Trapani sea salt is exported to Germany. If you come across an unrefined sea salt here or abroad then buy a couple of pounds, which should keep you going for a long time.

Sesame Seeds

These can be white, brown or black, and it is the more delicate white ones you will require here. Sometimes these are toasted to bring out their flavour, or used in conjunction with sesame oil.

Vegetables

Many vegetables come in small, medium and large; a small clove of garlic can be half or even one third of the size of a large one. So assume any vegetable is medium-sized unless the recipe states otherwise.

Vinegar

Most recipes call for a sherry vinegar or a good red wine vinegar. Keep a bottle of white wine vinegar to hand for acidulating water.

BASIC PREPARATIONS

Globe Artichokes

To turn an artichoke, equip yourself with a small paring knife and a bowl with some lemon juice or vinegar in it. Place a kitchen bin close by. Cut off the stalk from the artichoke and, starting at the base, cut away the coarse outer leaves, dipping the exposed flesh in the lemon juice or vinegar as you work to prevent it discolouring. When you have cut around the sides, slice off the top to about ½ inch/1 cm above the choke. Alternatively the choke can be cut out at this stage: scrape away the pitted layer where the choke was rooted to the heart using a teaspoon – it rapidly discolours on exposure to air. Tidy the sides and the base, taking care to remove all the tough stalk and dark green parts. Leave the artichoke heart in the lemon juice or vinegar until you are ready to cook it.

To cook the artichoke, bring a large pan of water to the boil, acidulate it with the lemon juice or vinegar the artichokes are in, and cook the hearts for 20 minutes. Cool them in a basin of cold water. Pull out the inner artichoke leaves, and use a teaspoon to remove the fibrous choke if you have not already done so. It should come away quite easily. If it is stubborn and will not come loose, it may require a little further cooking. Trim the heart so it looks tidy.

Bouquet Garni

A bouquet garni can either be tied together or enclosed in a small piece of muslin. Used to aromatize a dish, it consists of a few sprigs of parsley, a sprig of thyme and a bay leaf. Rosemary can be added for Provençal dishes.

Chopping Herbs

Chopped herbs need to be fresh; they quickly lose their flavour and the following day you will find they have little smell or taste. In my opinion frozen herbs are a disaster, but thyme, rosemary and bay are satisfactory dried. A glut of basil can be preserved in olive oil for several weeks.

It is worth mastering the process of finely chopping herbs, so that it becomes quick and easy. For leafy herbs, strip the leaves from the stalks and wash them. Take a large chopping board and a large, sharp knife, and with several rapid strokes of the knife break the pile of herbs down. Start at one end of the pile and work towards the other side, chopping them finely. You need to hold the tip of the knife steady against the chopping board with one hand, and chop as rapidly as possible, like a lever action, with the other hand.

When you have chopped the pile once, repeat the process twice more. If you are chopping parsley or some other leaf where the chopped pile is evidently quite wet, wrap it in a clean tea-towel or piece of muslin and squeeze out any excess water.

Clarified Butter

Clarified butter can be heated to a much higher temperature than ordinary butter. When butter is melted it separates into a clear yellow liquid and a milky residue which sinks. It is these milk particles which are responsible for ordinary butter burning at a much lower temperature. To prepare clarified butter, melt some butter in a pan, skim off the surface foam, and decant the crystal yellow liquid, the clarified butter. Discard the milky residue or stir it into soups or sauces.

Croûtons

Make croûtons on the day they are to be used. Thinly slice some day-old French bread, or remove crusts and cut slices into small cubes if this is more appropriate. Heat some olive oil or clarified butter in a frying pan to a depth of several millimetres. Test a small piece of bread to see whether the oil is hot enough – it should be enveloped by bubbles. Fry the croûtons on both sides until they are golden brown, then cool them on parchment paper.

If the croûtons are to accompany a particularly rich dish, or be spread with a rich substance, lay them on a baking sheet and place them in an oven heated to 180°C/350°F/Gas 4 for 5 minutes until they have dried out. With a pastry brush dab each side with olive oil or clarified butter and return them to the oven for another 10-12 minutes or until they are golden brown. Cool them on parchment paper before storing them.

Fines Herbes

A mixture of chopped parsley, chervil, tarragon and chives. I usually combine two parts parsley to one part chervil and chives and half of that of tarragon, which can be very pervasive. Chervil is one of those herbs which is never on call when it is needed, and is worth growing if you are able to.

Roasting and Grilling Peppers

If peppers are cooked under a grill or on a griddle, the skin will blister and blacken without the flesh overcooking. Performing the operation in the oven is considerably easier, but care has to be taken that the flesh does not overcook. They may not appear to be cooked after 15-20 minutes, but after they have been steamed in a closed plastic bag the skin should come away easily. If you cook them any longer in the oven the flesh will be too limp once they are cool.

Place the peppers on the grid of a grill pan in a very hot oven for 15-20 minutes. The skins should appear to be looser but not too black. Put one plastic carrier bag inside another and place the peppers inside. Seal the bag and leave them to cool. Once they are cool enough to handle, skin and deseed them, working over the open plastic bag or a bowl so as to retain the juices. They can be rinsed under running water to remove any traces of skin or seeds, and then patted dry, but avoid this if possible because it washes away the flavour of the juices.

Saffron

Saffron is precious and wonderful, but it does require careful handling to ensure that it gives its best to a dish. It is not a spice that should be used with gay abandon, as a dish can become 'medicinal' in character when it is excessive.

The finest saffron today comes from La Mancha in Spain. It might be graded as 'selecto', which is the very best, or extra, but usually the only indicator will be its place of origin. Filaments range in colour from paprika red through to a less desirable shade of yellow; their length and aroma will also account for quality. It stands to reason that broken or inferior filaments will be ground to a powder, so buying filaments is a guarantee of quality. As with most spices the flavour is strongest the minute it is ground. The most accurate way of quantifying saffron in a recipe is by an approximate number of filaments – pinches and quarter teaspoons can vary considerably.

To attain the full flavour and aroma from saffron filaments, first either roast them in a hot oven for 2-3 minutes or toast them in a dry frying pan for a minute or so until they darken slightly and become more brittle. Grind them and infuse with some boiling liquid for 10 minutes. Saffron loses its flavour after a period of cooking and is best added towards the end of slowly cooked dishes.

Tomatoes

Marmande, or beefsteak, tomatoes are ideal for 'concassée'. To skin and deseed them, cut a small cone from the top of each tomato, removing the core. Slash a small cross on the base of each fruit and plunge them into boiling water for 30 seconds. Dunk immediately into cold water – if you are doing a quantity, fill the sink. After a couple of minutes the skin will slip off and you can quarter them and remove the seeds, and cut them into small cubes.

If you are working with one or two tomatoes you may find it easier to skin them without blanching them. Quarter and deseed the tomato; with the skin face down on the chopping board, run a sharp thin-bladed knife between the flesh and the skin. This method also has an advantage over blanching in that there is no risk of cooking the surface flesh of the fruit; if the tomatoes are especially ripe this can be a problem.

Vegetable Stock

I have come to rely on the prepared fresh stocks to be found in Sainsbury stores; they come in $^1/_2$ pint/300 ml cartons of double strength, perfect when you need a small quantity here and there. Deborah Madison gives detailed instructions on how to produce different end flavours in *The Greens Cookbook*. You can make a basic stock by cutting into cubes some onion, leek, carrot, celery, a little fennel, aubergine, celeriac and courgette; sweat this in some butter or oil for 10 minutes, and if you are adding wine do so now and cook it for a couple of minutes. Lentils, garlic cloves and herbs can be included, and salt and white peppercorns. Cover with water and simmer for 35-45 minutes, skimming if necessary. Strain the stock straight away; once it is cool the surface fat can be removed easily.

Quinoa

Quinoa was a staple of the Incas, and is a tiny grain the size of couscous when cooked. Boil it as you would rice, for 15 minutes. Some supermarkets stock it, otherwise try health food stores.

COOKING EQUIPMENT

Cake Tins

The most useful cake tins are the 'springform' variety, with a removable collar which clips on to the base. Keep a range of these in sizes varying from 7 to 10 inches/18 to 25 cm. You should also have a range of tart tins with removable bases.

Chopping Boards

Keep several hard wood chopping boards: two small boards (one for fruit, one for garlic and shallots), and a large one, about 22 x 14 inches/60 x 35 cm, to be used for all other food preparation.

Griddle Plate

This is a basic ridged iron grid which fits over a single gas ring on the stove. Keep it clean with a minimum of detergent; take a wire brush to it if necessary. It should be dried thoroughly to prevent it rusting. If during the process of cooking food sticks to the grill and burns, let the griddle cool and clean it before continuing. If you are grilling a quantity of food you are also going to create a quantity of smoke, so a powerful extractor fan, or an open window, is advisable.

Knives

A good set of chef's knives is essential for preparing food. The knives should range in size from a heavy-duty chopping knife with a 10-12 inch/25-30 cm blade, through to a small paring knife. A bendy filleting knife and serrated bread knife are also of use. Good knives last a lifetime, and a feel for their use becomes second nature, in fact finding yourself without them in a strange kitchen can be quite disconcerting. Most blades today are stainless steel, and preferable to carbon steel which, though it sharpens to a finer edge, wears down more quickly and oxidizes to a grimy black. These should be greased when not in use to prevent their rusting: all a bit of a palaver. Sabatier knives are the most widely available knives for sale. A number of companies are licenced to produce them but only about four of these actually make decent knives. The Sabatier 'Jeune' knives which carry the grape emblem are perhaps the most common and of a good quality. But finest in reputation are the German knives: Dreizack, Dick and Victorinox are to be recommended, in that order of preference. David Mellor in Sloane Square, London, stocks Dreizack knives; they also have a catalogue and mail order service. There is an element of personal taste in knives, and it is as well to spend a little time handling different makes before you launch into the purchase of any one range.

Mandolin

A mandolin consists of two adjustable blades held within a wooden or steel frame. A folding support holds the mandolin at a tilt while slicing. The wooden models are not as effective. The stainless steel models are relatively expensive, but durable, and quite apart from their practical use of thinly slicing vegetables or controlling the thickness of a slice, they are a beautifully designed instrument.

Microwave

Scares and scandals continue to haunt the microwave. I acquired one in order to heat small amounts of food for my baby, and found it quite useful for melting butter and chocolate. I will gladly debate the disadvantages of cooking food in a microwave. Cooking food involves a series of chemical reactions, and the time something is cooked for is an important element. Cooking a dish in a microwave does not allow flavours to develop and mingle as they would if it was conventionally cooked.

Mouli-Légumes

This is useful when you want to purée food and indispensable for potatoes. The food will retain some texture rather than reducing to a totally smooth purée. However, for small quantities the hassle of dismantling the apparatus, washing it and reassembling it far outweighs its usefulness. The alternative is to reduce the food to a coarse purée in a food processor, potatoes excepted, and then pass it through a sieve. A sieve-pusher resembling a hand-held garden roller can be employed here, or a wooden mushroom, similar to the gadget your grandmother might have darned socks with.

Oven

I am sometimes quite alarmed at how differently ovens behave: pockets of heat may be concentrated in different parts of the oven, some ovens start off at the right temperature and then steadily rise, or fall; the number of baking sheets in the oven can affect the temperature and circulation of air, and if you cook three cakes rather than one you may get radically different results. When a recipe 'does not work' it might be for a number of reasons. All these recipes have been tested in a fan-assisted electric oven, so all I can offer is continuity, and if the first recipes you try differ in cooking times from those I have given then adjust the time in future.

Pestle and Mortar

Where possible spices should be freshly ground. This takes seconds: a pestle and mortar is essential.

Petal Steamer

This is a small steamer which fits inside a saucepan, and is extremely useful for steaming a small quantity of food. I keep one of these and a larger tiered steamer.

Saucepans

Next in importance after knives are saucepans. A good set of heavy-bottomed stainless steel saucepans lasts a lifetime. Bourgeat pans are excellent, and are available from professional stockists. The base of the pans is heavier than the domestic equivalent, food is less likely to catch and burn, and heat is more evenly distributed.

Scales

Electronic scales will give the greatest accuracy and some will allow you to weigh food to the nearest $1/8$ oz or gram. When I set out to buy some new scales recently, and tested a number in the shop for accuracy, most were up to 1 oz out; even the weights that came with the old-fashioned scales were $1/2$ oz/30g out. So if you are buying new scales it is worth taking a packet of food with you of which you know the weight, and testing several.

Nisbets offer a mail order service for professional kitchen equipment, including Bourgeat saucepans and a good selection of knives. Call 0272 555843 for a catalogue.

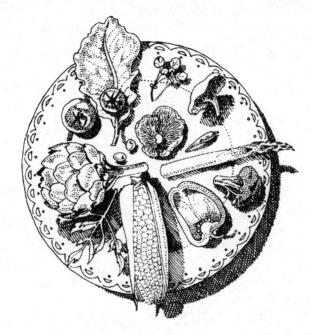

Chilled and Hot Soups

Gazpacho

Some would argue that a good gazpacho should be down-right brutish, and might find this version a touch too feeble; but I can happily eat this for lunch without feeling like Bluebeard for the rest of the day. It renders a smooth, red soup, and since no additional liquid is added to the vegetables, it is sweet and well-flavoured. For those who believe that the brute is the essence of a gazpacho, simply step up the garlic and onion, and omit the blanching.

Alice B. Toklas, in her wonderful cookery book, traces the origins of the gazpacho after being served very different versions of it in Málaga, Seville, Córdoba and Segovia. She concludes that it is related to the Polish *chlodnik*, the Turkish *caçik* and the Greek *tarata*, and that by some route of conquest it was handed from one Mediterranean spot to another, evolving in the process. The most interesting version is reported from Santiago de Chile in South America, where a Chilean writer, Señora Marta Brunet, tells of a gazpacho eaten by Spanish muleteers.

'These muleteers,' she says, 'carry with them on their journey-ings a flat earthenware dish – and garlic, olive oil, tomatoes and cucumbers, also dry bread which they crumble. Between two stones by the wayside they grind the garlic with a little salt and then add the oil. This mixture is rubbed all round the inside of the earthenware vessel. Then they slice the tomatoes and cucumbers and put alternating layers of each in the dish, inter-spersing the layers with layers of breadcrumbs and topping off the four tiers with more breadcrumbs and more oil. This done and prepared, they take a wet cloth, wrap it round the dish and leave it in a sunny place. The evaporation cooks the contents and when the cloth is dry the meal is ready. Too simple, my dear Watson.'

I should love to try this curiosity and hope, if I ever happen to be in that corner of the world, that I meet a Spanish muleteer who offers to make it for me.

This particular recipe produces a thick soup, which personally I like, but it can be thinned with a little tomato juice should you wish. The purpose of the double process of first puréeing the soup in the food processor, then passing it through a mouli-légumes, is to achieve a certain texture. Gazpacho is at its best freshly made, so prepare it as close to serving as possible.

---

3 small red peppers
1 1/2 cucumbers
3lb/1.4kg very ripe marmande
  tomatoes
1/2 red onion
2 garlic cloves, chopped

6 tablespoons best Italian extra
  virgin olive oil
2 dessertspoons aged red wine
  vinegar
salt, pepper

Accompaniment

ciabatta or a coarse-textured white bread
best Italian extra virgin olive oil

Preheat the oven on its highest setting. Roast the peppers on the rack of a grill pan for 20 minutes. The skins should appear to be loose without being too black. Place one plastic bag inside another and place the peppers inside. Seal the bag and leave them to cool. Once cold enough to handle, skin and deseed them, working over the open plastic bag so as to retain the juice. If necessary, rinse them under running water to remove traces of skin and seeds.

Peel and deseed the cucumbers, and cut into pieces. Cut a small cone from the top of each tomato to remove the core, and cut a cross on the base; plunge them into boiling water for 30 seconds then straight away into cold water. Skin, deseed and coarsely chop them. Coarsely chop the onion and blanch it for 45 seconds, then cool in cold water. Place all the ingredients for the soup into the bowl of a food processor (this may have to be done in stages). Strain any reserved pepper juice on to the vegetables. Reduce them to a coarse purée and pass this through a mouli-légumes. Season the soup and chill it for a couple of hours.

Serve the soup in bowls with the bread, dipping it into olive oil and then into the soup as you go – essential, since a gazpacho usually incorporates the bread in the soup itself.

Vichyssoise

Vichyssoise is made with potatoes, leeks and lots of cream. It is rich and velvety in texture, and very delicate in flavour. It has always passed as a 'party soup', but to glamorize it further, slice the white part of a leek into lengths 1½ inches/4cm long then slit these to the centre and cut the layers into thin strips. Heat some arachide oil and deep-fry the strips until they are lightly golden, which will take 1 or 2 minutes only. Drain them on kitchen paper and sprinkle them with salt. When you come to serve the soup, scatter over the chives and place a pile of the crispy leek strips in the centre.

1lb/450g potatoes	*1½ pints/900ml water*
10oz/285g white of leek	*2 parsley stalks*
2 sticks celery heart	*salt, white pepper, nutmeg*
2oz/55g unsalted butter	*½ pint/300ml single cream*

To garnish

finely chopped chives
deep-fried leek strips (see above)

Peel the potatoes and cook in salted water for 15 minutes or until cooked. Strain and press through a sieve.

Slit the leeks and celery lengthwise and slice them. Melt the butter in a saucepan and sweat these for 12-15 minutes over a very low heat. They should not colour, so stir them often.

Add 1½ pints/900ml of water together with the parsley stalks. Season with salt, pepper and nutmeg and simmer the soup, covered, for 20 minutes. Remove the parsley and liquidize the soup. Whisk in the puréed potato. Pass through a fine-mesh sieve. Stir in the cream, adjust the seasoning and chill. Serve sprinkled with the chopped chives and a pile of leek strips if wished.

Chilled Wild Garlic, Potato and Saffron Soup

I was as excited about tasting wild garlic, or ramsons, for the first time as I was when I first tasted rocket. With pungent leaves which look like lily-of-the-valley and beautiful white stellate flowers, it announces itself on the breeze long before you can see it, and grows profusely in damp and shady woods during the spring. Remember where it grows and you can dig the bulbs during the winter; these are also delicious. The flavour of wild garlic is more refined than ordinary garlic – it is not as strong. The whole leaf, stalk and flower can be used, in fact in much the same way as rocket. A lunch of warm new potatoes tossed with lots of chopped wild garlic, olive oil and white wine is my idea of springtime heaven. Or chop it finely and add to a mayonnaise, use it to make garlic butter, or throw some at the last minute into sautéed vegetables, potatoes or pasta.

The chlorophyll in the wild garlic rather upstages the saffron in terms of colour in this soup, but the honeyed flavour of the spice is still present as a backdrop.

8oz/225g wild garlic
15 saffron filaments
1 onion
12oz/340g potato
1¹/₂oz/45g unsalted butter

1 tablespoon olive oil
1¹/₂ pints/900ml water
salt, pepper
8fl oz/225ml single cream
lemon or lime juice

Reserve some of the garlic flowers as a garnish, then remove and discard the remaining flowers and chop the leaves and stalks. Roast the saffron for 1 minute in a dry frying pan and grind it, then infuse it with 1 tablespoon of boiling water for 10 minutes.

Peel and chop the onion, peel and cube the potato, heat the butter and oil in a saucepan and sweat these for 4-5 minutes. Add the water and bring to the boil, cover and simmer for 10 minutes. Liquidize the base of the soup, return it to the pan, season and bring back to the boil. Add the wild garlic and saffron tincture and cook for 3-4 minutes. Liquidize the soup so it retains some texture rather than becoming totally smooth. Allow it to cool then chill it for several hours.

Before serving, stir in the cream, sharpen it with a squeeze of lemon or lime juice and adjust the seasoning. Scatter a few garlic flowers over each bowl of soup.

Butternut Squash Soup with Gruyère

The rich sweetness of butternut squash makes this soup intense and quite delectable, though completely different in character to a traditional pumpkin soup. The Gruyère cheese melts into a glorious gooey mass, and the little croûtons provide some crunch.

This soup is equally good served with chopped herbs, and a swirl of cream rather than the Gruyère and croûtons. Try a mixture of parsley, chives, chervil, watercress and sorrel.

Stock

2 onions	³/₄oz/20g *unsalted butter*
4 carrots	2¹/₂ pints/1.4 litres *water*
5 sticks celery	*bouquet garni*
2 leeks	*salt, pepper*

2lb/900g *butternut squash,*	6fl oz/175ml *double cream*
weight excluding skin and seeds	*freshly grated nutmeg*
1¹/₂oz/45g *unsalted butter*	*salt, pepper*

To serve

3 slices white bread, ¹/₄ inch/0.5cm thick
clarified butter
6-9oz/170-250g *Gruyère cheese*

To prepare the stock, skin the onions, then trim and chop all the vegetables, melt the butter in a saucepan and sweat them for 8 minutes. Add $2\frac{1}{2}$ pints/1.4 litres of water, the bouquet garni and seasoning, bring to the boil and simmer the stock for 20 minutes. Strain and discard the vegetables.

Slice the squash. Heat the butter in a saucepan and sweat it for 5 minutes. Add the stock and cook the soup for another 5 minutes. Purée it in a liquidizer, add the cream and season with nutmeg and more salt and pepper as necessary.

Remove the crusts from the bread and cut into small cubes. Heat some clarified butter in a frying pan and fry the croûtons to a golden brown, stirring them to ensure they cook evenly. Cool them on parchment paper. Grate the Gruyère.

Serve the soup piping hot, in bowls, with Gruyère scattered over, accompanied by the croûtons.

Borscht with Basil Chantilly

The bright vermilion of this borscht is very gratifying, served with a spoon of creamy chantilly with basil running through it, which melts over the top of the soup.

Borscht

2lb/900g raw beetroot	12oz/340g tomatoes, skinned,
1 large onion	seeded and chopped
3 sticks celery	3/4oz/20g sorrel
1 small bulb fennel	salt, pepper
1 1/2oz/45g unsalted butter	lemon juice
2 1/4 pints/1.3 litres water	

Basil chantilly

3fl oz/85ml double cream	a handful of basil leaves
3fl oz/85ml crème fraîche	

Wearing rubber gloves to avoid staining your hands, peel the beetroot and grate it using the fine grating blade of a food processor; alternatively grate it by hand.

Peel the onion and chop it. Trim the celery and fennel and chop also. Heat the butter in a saucepan and sweat these over a medium heat for 10 minutes.

Add the beetroot to the pan and cover with 2¼ pints/1.3 litres of water. Bring the soup to the boil and simmer it for 5 minutes, then add the tomato and cook for another 5 minutes. Prepare a chiffonade of the sorrel, add it to the soup, and cook until the sorrel turns a dull green. Purée the soup in a liquidizer, return it to the pan and season, adding lemon juice to taste. Plenty of salt and lemon are required to achieve the correct balance.

Whip the double cream and crème fraîche together until they form soft peaks. Finely chop the basil so you have 1 heaped dessertspoon and stir this into the cream. Serve the soup with a dollop of the basil chantilly in the centre.

Tomato Soup

This soup gracefully heralds the start to any meal. Its quality is dependent on the tomatoes being sweet and ripe: perfect for late summer days when plum tomatoes are in season. It is a simple, fresh soup with no added stock.

5 shallots	*bouquet garni*
6lb/3kg ripe tomatoes	*1 level teaspoon caster sugar*
2oz/55g unsalted butter	*salt, pepper*

To serve

flat-leaf parsley, finely chopped

Finely chop the shallots. Wash and slice the tomatoes. Melt the butter in a large saucepan with a tight-fitting lid. Sweat the shallots for a few minutes until they are translucent and soft. Add the tomatoes, the bouquet garni, the sugar and seasoning. Cover the pan tightly with a lid and cook the contents over a very low heat for 30-40 minutes, stirring occasionally.

Remove the bouquet garni, liquidize the soup and pass it through a sieve back into the pan. Reheat it, adjust the seasoning and serve with a little chopped parsley sprinkled over.

Minestrone with Olive Oil and Parmesan

Everyone, it would seem, loves minestrone. In Italy there are many regional variations and this particular version is a hybrid with no special geographical identity. It is based on the recipe in Anna del Conte's *Secrets from an Italian Kitchen*.

One qualifying feature of a minestrone is its long slow cooking: 2 or 3 hours. The cooked soup is thick, verging on a stew. It is worth cooking a cauldron-sized amount of minestrone; you can dip into the left-overs when midnight hunger strikes. The Italians eat it cold for lunch throughout the baking summer months: its preparation begins first thing in the morning and by lunchtime it is cooked and cooled to perfection.

Minestrone provides a good extra virgin olive oil with the perfect stage to reveal its full glory. The Sicilian Ravida oil is a personal favourite, and turns this soup into something very special. The pepperiness provided by such an oil dispenses with the need for any additional pepper.

---

2 carrots
1 potato
4oz/115g celeriac, weight
   excluding skin
1 small aubergine
8oz/225g courgette
4oz/115g green beans
1 stick celery
2 leeks
4oz/115g shelled peas

1 marmande tomato, skinned,
   seeded and chopped
4 pints/2.2 litres water
4 tablespoons extra virgin olive oil
2 garlic cloves
salt
4oz/115g macaroni
1oz/30g vermicelli, broken into
   1 inch/2cm lengths
6oz/170g young spinach leaves

Pesto

1oz/30g basil leaves	*2 garlic cloves*
1oz/30g flat-leaf parsley	*1 tablespoon extra virgin olive oil*

To serve

extra virgin olive oil
freshly grated Parmesan

Peel the carrots and potato and cut into neat $^1/_2$ inch/1cm cubes. Also cube the celeriac, aubergine and courgette. Trim the beans and cut into 1 inch/2cm lengths, and trim and slice the celery and leeks. Place these vegetables with the peas and tomato in a large pan along with the water, olive oil, and garlic cloves, sliced. Add some salt and simmer the soup, uncovered, for at least 2 hours.

To prepare the pesto, finely chop the herbs and garlic together. Place them in a pestle and mortar with the olive oil and crush, as far as possible, to a paste.

Some 20 minutes before the minestrone is to be served, add the pasta and the spinach leaves. Stop cooking the soup while the macaroni is still firm to the bite. Stir in the pesto and allow it to stand for a few minutes. Adjust the seasoning.

Serve the minestrone with a generous addition of olive oil to each serving, and accompany it with a bowl of Parmesan.

Pistou

Pistou is the Provençal relation of minestrone. They are both hearty vegetable soups with many features in common, but are totally different in character.

---

2 *carrots*	8oz/225g *haricot beans, soaked*
4oz/115g *turnips*	*overnight*
1 *large potato*	5 *pints/2.8 litres water*
2 *sticks celery*	*salt, pepper*
2 *leeks*	*generous pinch of saffron filaments*
4oz/115g *pumpkin or other*	8oz/225g *French beans*
squash, weight excluding skin	2oz/55g *vermicelli, broken*
4oz/115g *shelled peas*	*into* 1/2 *inch/1cm lengths*

Pistou

---

3 *tablespoons tomato purée*	4fl oz/115ml *extra virgin*
4 *garlic cloves*	*olive oil*
1 1/2oz/45g *basil*	

Chapons

---

6 *slices French bread* 1/2 *inch/1cm*	1 *garlic clove*
thick	*olive oil*

To serve

freshly grated Parmesan

Peel and cube the carrots, turnips and potato. Trim and slice the celery and leeks. Cube the pumpkin. Place these vegetables together with the peas and haricot beans in a large saucepan, add 5 pints/2.8 litres of water and seasoning. Bring to the boil and simmer uncovered for 50 minutes.

Toast the saffron for 1 minute in a dry frying pan until dry and brittle, then grind it and infuse with 1 tablespoon of boiling water for 10 minutes. Place all the ingredients for the pistou into the bowl of a food processor and reduce to a paste.

Trim and cut the French beans into 1 inch/2cm lengths. Add the saffron tincture, beans and vermicelli to the soup and cook for 10 minutes longer.

Toast the bread, rub each slice with the garlic clove and trickle over a little olive oil.

Stir a ladle of the soup into the pistou then pour it back into the soup; adjust seasoning. Place a chapon on the bottom of each diner's bowl and ladle soup over. Accompany with a bowl of freshly grated Parmesan.

French Onion Soup 'Gratinée'

Quite irresistible: thin and dark with the caramel from slowly cooked onions, a splash of Armagnac and some toasted sourdough bread floating in it, with bubbling cheese running into the soup like a river of lava.

2lb/900g Spanish onions
2oz/55g unsalted butter
5fl oz/150ml dry white wine
2¼ pints/1.2 litres vegetable
  stock
salt, pepper

12 pieces sourdough bread,
  2 inches/5cm square and
  ¼ inch/0.5cm thick
5oz/140g Gruyère, grated
2oz/55g Cheddar, grated
Armagnac or brandy

Peel and halve the onions and slice thinly. Heat the butter in two separate frying pans or heavy-bottomed saucepans and cook the onions over a very low heat for 1 hour, stirring regularly so that they reduce without colouring. Combine the onions in one saucepan, turn the heat up high and cook for a further 15-20 minutes, stirring frequently, until deeply golden. Add the wine and cook for 1-2 minutes. Add the stock and seasoning, bring to the boil, cover and simmer for 30 minutes. Adjust seasoning.

Toast the bread. Combine the cheeses and pile thickly on to the toast. Ladle the soup into bowls, pour some Armagnac into a cup and with your fingertips splash a little into each bowl. Float a couple of toasts in each one and place the bowls under the grill until the cheese is bubbling and running into the soup.

Watercress Soup

Deep grass green, pungent and peppery, this soup has featured at Le Gavroche, 43 Upper Brook Street, London W1 for the last twenty years. It consists simply of watercress, potato and water and takes about 10 minutes to cook. There is an art to the preparation which leaves the chlorophyll intact. The watercress is cooked in butter very quickly, finely sliced potato is added, and then boiling water so that it comes to the boil and cooks immediately. Serve hot or chilled.

1¹/₂oz/45g unsalted butter
10oz/285g watercress leaves, with
* minimal stalk*
8oz/225g potato, peeled and finely
* sliced*

2 pints/1.1 litre boiling water
salt, pepper

To serve

double cream
diced croûtons (¹/₄ inch/0.5cm), fried in clarified butter

Melt the butter in a saucepan and cook the watercress briefly until just wilted. Add the potato and cook 1 minute longer. Add the boiling water, bringing to the boil immediately, then season and cook for 6 minutes. Liquidize and pass through a fine-mesh sieve; adjust seasoning. Serve with a swirl of cream and the croûtons.

Sweetcorn Soup with Tarragon Crisps

Freshly made tarragon crisps with sweetcorn soup are the inspiration of Philip Howard at The Square, 32 King Street, London SW1. He always serves his soups with an interesting little accompaniment, something creamy which will melt into the soup or something crunchy on the side. The soup is delicious with or without its accompaniment. If you do not have time to make your own crisps then cheat: buy some Kettle Chips and paint these with the tarragon butter.

---

5 corn cobs
2oz/55g unsalted butter
5oz/140g shallots, finely chopped

1³/4 pints/1 litre vegetable stock
  or water
salt, pepper
freshly grated nutmeg

To serve

double cream

Strip the corn kernels from the cob using a knife. Melt the butter in a saucepan and sweat the shallots over a low heat for 4 minutes. Add the corn, turn the heat up to medium and cook for 5 minutes, stirring occasionally. Add the stock, bring to the boil and simmer for 12 minutes; season with salt, pepper and nutmeg. Liquidize and pass through a sieve. Reheat, adjust seasoning and serve with a swirl of cream.

Tarragon Crisps

---

arachide oil for deep-frying
1 large red Desirée potato, cut into
   1mm slices (or a baking potato)
$2^{1}/_{2}oz/75g$ unsalted butter

3oz/85g shallots, finely chopped
$^{1}/_{2}oz/15g$ tarragon, chopped
$^{1}/_{2}$ teaspoon salt

Heat the oil until medium hot. Rinse and dry the potato slices and deep-fry in batches until uniformly golden. Drain and cool on kitchen paper. Melt 2oz/55g of the butter and sweat the shallots for 3 minutes, then add the tarragon and cook for a further 2 minutes. Stir in the remaining butter. Sieve the tarragon butter into a bowl and stir in the salt. Paint the crisps sparingly with melted butter just before serving.

See also:
Pasta and Bean Soup with Extra Virgin Olive Oil and Parmesan (page 139)

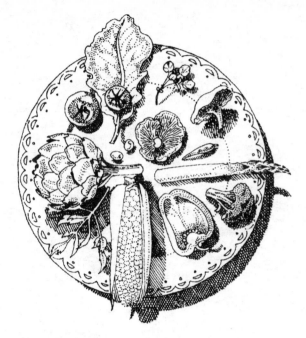

Salads and Mezze

Greek Salad

I suspect the dubious reputation of the Greek salad is not so much to do with the actual concept as with the fact that if you visit Greece you are expected to eat it twice a day for the duration of your stay.

There are a few rules or guidelines which act as stardust for this salad: use a high quality extra virgin olive oil, feta made from ewe's or goat's milk, 'Le Moulin' olives, and flavourful tomatoes such as marmande or plum. Should you have visited a Mediterranean country recently and returned with a large bunch of dried wild oregano, this too makes all the difference. Serve it with some coarse-textured white bread to soak up the juices.

1lb/450g tomatoes (marmande or plum)	*8oz/225g feta (ewe's or goat's milk)*
salt, pepper, caster sugar	*2oz/55g black olives, pitted*
1/2 large cucumber	*best extra virgin olive oil*
1 large red onion	*2 heaped teaspoons dried oregano*

Thickly slice the tomatoes, cutting across the fruit rather than down it, so as to discard the end slice with the core. Halve each slice if you are using marmande tomatoes. Place these on a serving dish and sprinkle them with salt, pepper and sugar. Leave them for 20 minutes until the juices run; this will take the place of vinegar or lemon juice.

Peel the cucumber, halve it lengthwise and scoop out the seeds with a teaspoon. Slice it into 1/2 inch/1cm crescents and reserve these in a dish. Peel the onion, halve it downwards and slice thinly into crescents.

Arrange the tomatoes, cucumber and onion together on the serving dish. Slice the feta and place it on top, and scatter over the olives. Trickle over plenty of olive oil and sprinkle with oregano.

Moroccan Salad

At some point in history it would seem that gazpacho made the crossing from Cádiz to Tangier, evolving on the journey to Morocco. Paula Wolfert explains the link between this salad and gazpacho in her book *Good Food from Morocco*. Gazpacho, which in Arabic means 'soaked bread', was imported to Spain by the Moors and consisted of garlic, bread, lemon juice, olive oil, salt and water. When Columbus discovered America in the same year that the Moors finally departed from Spain, tomatoes and peppers were added to the basic Moorish preparation and a range of Spanish gazpachos evolved. In turn tomatoes and peppers found their way over to Morocco and became a mainstay of salads there. Friends recently returned from Morocco said they were served this salad almost daily as a first course: I can imagine few dishes as adept at countering a searing heat. Like a gazpacho the salad is served chilled, and it is a very clean, refreshing dish, sharp with lemon juice which is added in high proportion to the olive oil.

Peppers can be effectively skinned by a short roasting in a hot oven, followed by steaming them in a sealed plastic bag. This ensures an even cooking and slackens the flesh in a fashion particularly appropriate to Italian and Provençal salads. Here they are best grilled, either on a griddle or under a conventional grill, then steamed in a sealed bag. The flesh remains firm which, in this instance, is more appropriate.

The salad can be accompanied by bruschetta. Toast some day-old coarse-textured white bread, ideally on a griddle. Give it a cursory rub with a clove of garlic and lightly douse it with extra virgin olive oil. 'Salty' additions like olives, sun-dried tomatoes, goat's cheese or feta will also fit in nicely.

2 *green peppers*	$^1/_2$ *teaspoon chilli, finely chopped*
2 *red peppers*	1 *heaped tablespoon flat-leaf*
1 *cucumber*	*parsley, finely chopped*
6 *spring onions*	*dried oregano (optional)*
2 *marmande tomatoes*	

Dressing

1 *large garlic clove*	*pepper*
salt	6 *tablespoons extra virgin olive oil*
2 *tablespoons lemon juice*	

Grill the peppers on a griddle or under a conventional grill, turning them as the skin starts to blacken and cooking on all sides. Place one plastic bag inside another, place the peppers inside, seal and leave them to steam while they cool. Remove the skin and seeds and if necessary rinse the flesh. Cut into strips 2 inches/5cm long by $^1/_4$ inch/0.5cm.

Peel and deseed the cucumber, and cut into strips the same size as the pepper. Trim the spring onions and cut into thin 2 inches/5cm strips. Quarter the tomatoes, seed them and skin them by placing the skin side of each quarter face down on the chopping board and running a thin-bladed knife between the skin and the flesh. Cut into strips to match the other vegetables and place all these together in a salad bowl with the chilli. Cover and chill this for a couple of hours, but do not place it in the coldest part of the refrigerator – it needs to be fairly cold but not icy. If your refrigerator is a cold one, remove the salad 30 minutes before serving.

To prepare the dressing, crush the garlic clove with $^1\!/_2$ teaspoon of salt using the flat of a knife until it forms a paste. Whisk this with the lemon juice and some pepper. Add the olive oil.

Just before serving, pour the dressing over the salad, stir in the parsley and adjust seasoning. Serve with a pinch of dried oregano sprinkled over.

Salad of Grilled Vegetables

This salad is singularly Mediterranean and shouts 'summer'. Grilled vegetables were part of the Italianate revolution of the 1980s; few fads in food can have been more welcome for the vegetarian. Smoky in flavour, the flesh becomes slack and silky, impregnated with olive oil. If you are leaving the cooked vegetables for any time, layer with herbs and more oil. You will need a griddle (see page 11) for this recipe, and expect to generate a considerable amount of smoke: so unless your extractor fan is super-efficient, shut yourself into the kitchen and open the window.

extra virgin olive oil	6 flat-cap mushrooms
salt, pepper	1 large red onion
1 aubergine	4 tomatoes (ideally plum tomatoes)
2 red peppers	$^{1}/_{2}oz/15g$ rocket
2 garlic cloves	4oz/115g black olives
2 courgettes	

Heat the griddle. As you grill the vegetables brush them with olive oil and season them. The vegetables are cooked as they start to juice and become charred in patches; reserve them separately.

Thickly slice the aubergine, and grill the slices on both sides.

Preheat the oven to 200°C/400°F/Gas 6. Remove the tops and seeds from the peppers and quarter them. Grill these, then place them in a small baking dish, finely chop the garlic and scatter it over the peppers. Trickle over a little more olive oil and bake them for 15 minutes.

Slice the courgettes on the bias into strips about 3 inches/8cm long and grill these on both sides. Trim the mushroom stalks level with the caps and cook the caps on both sides, grilling the cupped surface first so that when you grill the other side you can reserve any juices. Peel the onion, halve and cut into wedges, and cook these also. Halve the tomatoes, and grill them cut side first, then skin side.

To assemble the salad, arrange all the vegetables attractively either on individual plates or one large one, including any juices that have been given out. Tuck the rocket leaves and olives in here and there. Trickle over some more olive oil.

Chopped Olives on Bruschetta with a Salad of Rocket, Watercress and Parmesan

Peppery and pungent leaves, fine shavings of Parmesan, the olives are coarsely chopped and mixed with tomato, and piled on to garlic toast. This is a simple dish; it is quick to prepare and can be lovely providing all the individual ingredients are lovely – good olives, ripe tomatoes, a decent oil and so forth.

12oz/340g black olives
3 plum tomatoes
extra virgin olive oil
lemon juice
4oz/115g rocket, watercress and
  radicchio

salt, pepper
1¹/₂oz/45g Parmesan, finely
  shaved
4 slices bread, ¹/₂ inch/1cm thick
1 garlic clove

Stone the olives and coarsely chop them. Skin the plum tomatoes by blanching them, then plunge them into cold water. Dice these, without removing the seeds, and mix with the olives. Add 2 tablespoons of olive oil and a good squeeze of lemon juice.

Wash the salad leaves and place them in a bowl. Dress with olive oil, season and toss in the Parmesan shavings. Toast the bread, rub it with the garlic clove and trickle over a little olive oil. Place some of the olive mixture over half of it with a pile of the salad to the side.

Aromatic Salad with Cauliflower and Almonds

This is a chunky salad; lamb's lettuce is present as a background leaf. Cauliflower and artichoke are poached in an aromatic broth flavoured with saffron, or *à la Grècque*, and the reduced liquor forms the basis of the vinaigrette. This salad is a striking combination of red, yellow and green.

---

2 red peppers
10fl oz/275ml water
2fl oz/55ml extra virgin olive oil
   plus another 4 tablespoons
juice of ¹/₂ lemon
1 garlic clove, finely chopped
2 shallots, finely chopped
1 teaspoon salt
¹/₃ teaspoon each of coriander seeds,
   black peppercorns, fennel seeds,
   tied into a muslin sachet

bouquet garni (see page 7)
15 saffron filaments, roasted and
   ground (see page 9)
2 artichoke hearts, sliced (reserve
   in lemon juice until required,
   see page 6)
9oz/250g cauliflower, cut into
   ¹/₂ inch/1cm florets
black pepper
4oz/115g lamb's lettuce
1oz/30g flaked almonds, toasted

Preheat the oven to 200°C/400°F/Gas 6 and cook the peppers for 20 minutes. Place one plastic bag inside another and contain the peppers inside. Put aside to steam and cool; remove the skin and seeds and cut into strips. Prepare an aromatic broth: combine in a saucepan the water, the 2fl oz/55ml of olive oil, lemon juice, garlic, shallots, salt, spices and bouquet garni. Bring to the boil, simmer, covered, for 10 minutes. Infuse the saffron in 1 tablespoon of boiling water.

Add the saffron tincture to the pan, with the artichoke and cauliflower; bring to the boil and cook, covered, for 4 minutes. Remove the vegetables and reduce the remaining liquor to about 3 tablespoons. Strain, and add the 4 tablespoons of olive oil once cool; season with pepper and salt if necessary.

To serve, toss the lamb's lettuce, cauliflower, artichoke and red pepper with the dressing. Mound on plates and scatter the almonds over.

Salad of Lamb's Lettuce, Artichoke and Parmesan

'The Square', in London's St James's, serves food just as I like it – there is no elaborate presentation and great care is taken to maximize flavours. Whenever I have eaten there the dishes have been faultless. This salad was among them. Part of its charm lies with the interesting combination of flavours. As with the salad above, lamb's lettuce is included as a supporting ingredient – it is not a 'leafy' salad as such.

3 red peppers	3oz/85g lamb's lettuce
6 globe artichokes	2¹/₂oz/70g Parmesan

Dressing

1 dessertspoon sherry vinegar	6 dessertspoons extra virgin olive oil
1 scant teaspoon salt, pepper	
1 level teaspoon mustard	2 dessertspoons hazelnut oil

Heat the oven to 200°C/400°F/Gas 6 and roast the peppers for 20 minutes. Place one plastic bag inside another, place the peppers inside, seal the bag and leave them to steam as they cool for several hours. Remove the skin and seeds, working over the open bag so as to collect the juices. Cut the peppers into strips and strain the juices over them.

Pare the artichokes according to the instructions on page 6, leaving the choke intact, and boil them in acidulated water for 20 minutes. Drain and reserve them in cold water.

Wash and dry the lamb's lettuce with care; there is no need to twist off the base unless the little roots are present. Thinly shave the Parmesan, using a mandolin if you possess one. To prepare the dressing, whisk together the vinegar, salt, pepper and mustard, then whisk in the oils.

Remove the choke from the artichoke hearts, scrape out the pitted layer with a teaspoon and slice them. Toss the red pepper and artichoke with half of the dressing. Toss the lamb's lettuce with the remainder of the dressing. Gently combine these two, divide between individual plates and scatter some Parmesan shavings over.

Piquant Salad of Aubergine, Cucumber, Baby Corn and Sesame

The origins of this salad are Thai, but all the ingredients are readily available. Perhaps the most noteworthy curiosity is that almost no fat is involved – the presence of an oil would be out of place and would dull the overall piquancy. This is a truly delicious salad which can be successfully woven into a meal centred on Italian flavours.

If you do not possess a griddle for char-grilling the baby corn, simply brush them with oil as indicated, heat a cast-iron frying pan until it is smoking hot, then sear them until they are patched with colour on all sides.

1 tablespoon arachide oil	*3 shallots*
1 teaspoon dark sesame oil	*2 garlic cloves*
2 aubergines	*1 long red chilli*
1 cucumber	*2 tablespoons light soy sauce*
salt, caster sugar	*1 teaspoon caster sugar*
10 baby corn	*2 tablespoons lemon juice*
1¹/₂ level tablespoons white sesame	*a few basil leaves*
seeds	

Preheat the oven to 200°C/400°F/Gas 6. Mix the arachide oil with the sesame oil. Halve the aubergines lengthwise and make an incision around the outside of the flesh ¹/₄ inch/0.5cm inside the skin, paint the cut surface of each half with the oil and roast for 15-20 minutes until patched with brown. When they have cooled, using the original incision as a guide, cut out the flesh removing it in one piece. Slice diagonally into ³/₄ inch/1.5cm pieces and reserve in a bowl.

Peel the cucumber and discard the skin. Make a julienne of the cucumber ¹/₆ inch/0.25cm square, half the length of the cucumber. Discard the central core of seeds. Sprinkle the cucumber strips with salt and sugar and leave in a colander for 30 minutes to exude the juices. Rinse and drain them on kitchen paper or a tea-towel and place in the bowl with the aubergine.

Halve the baby corn lengthwise and brush with the sesame-arachide oil. Heat a griddle or cast-iron frying pan (see above), cook the corn until they are mottled with brown on both sides, and reserve them.

Heat a dry frying pan, toast the sesame seeds for a couple of minutes until lightly golden and reserve. Peel and coarsely chop the shallots and garlic cloves. Finely slice the chilli so you have 1 teaspoonful. Again in a dry frying pan over a low heat, cook these together for 5 minutes until they are quite limp but not coloured. Mince them finely with a large chopping knife then mix them in a bowl with the soy sauce, sugar and lemon juice.

To serve the salad, mix together the aubergine, cucumber and baby corn in a bowl, scatter over two-thirds of the sesame seeds and toss with the dressing. Either divide it among individual plates or mound on to one large one. Scatter over the remaining sesame seeds so they fall around the edge of the plate as well. Cut the basil leaves into thin strips and scatter over.

Crudités with a Walnut Chutney and a Herb Purée

There is a time of year, as winter goes into spring, that I crave crudités. Eating crudités and drinking iced drinks both have warm weather associations and both feel uncomfortable during colder months. Crudités are cleansing, they are very pure, and it goes without saying that they are also very good for you.

Serve a selection of vegetables, and store them in ice cold water once you have prepared them. If the vegetables are raw you could serve them on crushed ice. Choose from cauliflower, blanched green beans, sugar snaps or mangetouts, radishes, strips of red and yellow pepper, batons of courgette and carrot and quarters of young fennel bulbs. Crudités are largely a matter of taste. All manner of vegetables can be eaten raw; it really depends on what you like. You can also serve cooked baby potatoes and quarters of cooked beetroot.

The recipe for the chutney comes from Madhur Jaffrey's *A Taste of India*. I have combined Greek yoghurt with a thinner, plain yoghurt to give a richer, thicker chutney.

Walnut chutney

2oz/55g walnuts	2 tablespoons plain yoghurt
$^1/_4$ teaspoon salt	2 tablespoons Greek yoghurt
$^1/_4$ teaspoon cayenne pepper	

Grind the walnuts in an electric coffee grinder or mortar; they will reduce to a thick paste. Combine all the ingredients in a bowl and work until smooth, using a small whisk if necessary.

Herb purée

1oz/30g *coriander leaves*	1 *dessertspoon lemon juice*
³/₄oz/20g *basil leaves*	¹/₂ *teaspoon green chilli, chopped*
¹/₂oz/15g *flat-leaf parsley*	¹/₂ *garlic clove*
8 *tablespoons extra virgin olive oil*	*salt*

To prepare the herb purée, place all the ingredients in a liquidizer and reduce to a purée.

Mezze

The point of mezze is to have lots of little tasty dishes, contrasting and complementing each other. Apart from the tabbouleh, baba ghanoush and salad of radish and orange below, you could serve some bissara, the Moroccan purée of broad beans on page 135, or some hummus (page 136), and little deep-fried falafel (page 137). Serve plenty of pitta bread warm from the oven, rub the cut surfaces with garlic and sprinkle with more olive oil if wished.

Tabbouleh

Too often tabbouleh is dry and stodgy, made predominantly with bulgar wheat. Made with a large proportion of herbs it is pungent and fresh. Use tender young leaves, not older coarse ones, and just a smattering of wheat. There should be sufficient dressing to leave it wet, which is why the water is added at the end of this recipe.

3oz/85g bulgar wheat	*1$^{1}/_{2}$fl oz/45ml lemon juice*
2oz/55g flat-leaf parsley	*salt, pepper*
1oz/30g mint	*4$^{1}/_{2}$fl oz/125ml extra virgin*
6 spring onions	*olive oil*
8oz/225g cherry tomatoes	*2 tablespoons water*

Cover the bulgar wheat with plenty of boiling water and leave it to soak for 30 minutes. Drain and place it in a bowl. Wash the herbs and coarsely chop them. Trim and finely slice the spring onions. Quarter the cherry tomatoes. Mix these ingredients together. Whisk the lemon juice with the seasoning, add the olive oil and 2 tablespoons of water, and dress the salad.

Baba Ghanoush

This rather innocent looking purée is very gutsy, sharp with lemon, bitter with tahini and resonant with garlic. This method of grilling the aubergines gives the purée a crucial smokiness which you cannot achieve by cooking them under an ordinary grill, or in the oven. It is at its best eaten freshly made.

---

2 *aubergines*
1 *small garlic clove*
2 *dessertspoons light tahini*
juice of 1 small lemon
2 *tablespoons extra virgin olive oil*

$^1/_2$ *teaspoon cumin, freshly ground*
1 *heaped tablespoon flat-leaf*
  parsley, finely chopped
salt, pepper

To serve

extra virgin olive oil
flat-leaf parsley, finely chopped

Preheat the griddle, pierce the aubergines in a number of places to prevent them bursting, and cook on all sides until they are black and charred and the skin is blistering and peeling. When cool enough to handle remove the skin, place the flesh in a sieve and press out as much water as possible. Place in a food processor with the garlic and reduce to a textured purée.

Blend the tahini with the lemon juice and the oil, and combine this with the aubergine. Finally stir in the cumin and parsley and season with salt and pepper. Trickle over a little olive oil and a sprinkling of chopped parsley before serving.

Salad of Radish and Orange

This is not intended to be served as a salad in its own right, but it slots into a mezze as a clean and contrasting item. Its vibrant red and orange stands out, set between the muted shades of the other dishes.

4oz/115g radishes
  (leaves removed)
2 small oranges

lemon juice
salt, pepper

Wash and slice the radishes discarding end slices. Cut the skin and pith from the oranges and remove the segments by slicing between each one, leaving the pith which separates them. If the segments are thick, halve them. Combine the radish slices and orange segments in a bowl, sharpen with lemon juice and season with salt and pepper.

See also:
Salad 'Gribiche' (page 72)
Porcini Salad (page 95)
Warm Salad of Girolles with Rocket, Baby Spinach and a Mustard
    Mayonnaise (page 96)
Mushrooms à la Grècque with Herbs and Tomato (page 99)
Bruschetta with Parsley Pesto and Aubergine Salad (page 122)
Bissara (page 135)
Hummus (page 136)
Potato and Truffle Salad (page 207)
Warm Salad of Pappardelle with Herbs and Baby Spinach (page
    240)
Wild Rice Salad with Baby Corn, Coriander and Almonds (page
    254)

Eggs and Cheese

Eggs Florentine

Eggs Florentine were a permanent fixture on the menu of a restaurant where I once worked: in a bowl half full of frozen spinach, somewhere was hidden an egg; there was never any sight of the spinach, which was drowned in a sea of thin, lily-white béchamel, and the surface was a slick of bubbling, tasteless Cheddar. I suspect this version (which consists of a base of toasted brioche, lightly cooked fresh spinach, eggs poached the proper way, a few pan-fried mushrooms and a foamy hollandaise) does not take that much longer to prepare.

It makes an exotic brunch dish and is particularly delicious made with chanterelles or some other wild mushrooms. Do not be deterred if these are not available; shiitake or oyster mushrooms will do nicely. Avoid the waxy supermarket brioche which has too much sugar for savoury recipes; buy some from a proper bakery.

The method of preparing the hollandaise departs slightly from the traditional one. The eggs are whisked with some white wine into a sabayon before the butter is added. The result is lighter than usual and pleasantly sharp.

2lb/900g young spinach leaves	*vinegar*
2oz/55g unsalted butter	*6 eggs (size 2) (or 12 for a main*
8oz/225g mushrooms	*course)*
salt, pepper	*6 slices brioche*

Hollandaise

6oz/170g unsalted butter	*lemon juice*
2 egg yolks (size 2)	*salt*
2fl oz/55ml white wine	

Wash and dry the spinach between tea towels. You will need about 1oz/30g of butter to cook the spinach. Melt a small knob in a saucepan; when it is hot and the foam subsides throw in some leaves, and toss until they wilt. Cover the pan and cook for 1 minute. Remove to a bowl and cook the rest of the spinach in the same fashion. Wipe the mushrooms and cut or tear them into pieces if they are large.

To prepare the hollandaise, heat the butter in a saucepan until it is melted and bubbling. Place a double saucepan over a very low heat with about ½ inch/1cm of hot water in the bottom half and whisk the egg yolks in the top half of the boiler for 1-2 minutes, then add the white wine and continue whisking until you have a stable sabayon. Slowly whisk in the melted butter and season the sauce with lemon juice and salt. The hollandaise should keep for a couple of hours at room temperature – if it is kept in too warm a place it will curdle.

The eggs can be poached in an egg-poaching pan if you wish, alternatively bring a large pan of water to a trembling boil and acidulate it with vinegar. Take two cups and break an egg into each one. Stir the water with a long-handled spoon until you have a lazy whirlpool. Drop the eggs one at a time into the water. If your pan is large you can cook all the eggs in one go, otherwise do them in batches. As the eggs poach they will rise to the surface. Trim the ragged tendrils of white and discard; hopefully this will leave you with perfect teardrops, though quite often this is not the case. Allow them to cook a couple of minutes longer, then remove with a slotted spoon. They can be stored in iced water if not needed immediately, and reheated by plunging them into boiling water for just long enough to heat them through.

The recipe can be prepared in advance to this stage. To serve the eggs Florentine, melt some of the remaining butter in a frying pan and when it is hot and the foam subsides, cover the base with mushrooms and fry until they begin to colour. Remove them to a bowl and when they are all cooked, season them. Drain any excess fluid from the spinach, reheat and season it, and mix in the mushrooms. Toast the brioche. Place some spinach on top of the brioche, making a shallow well in the centre, nestle a poached egg in this, and spoon some hollandaise over.

Cheese Soufflé with Watercress

A special feature of this soufflé is the double lining of the soufflé mould, which creates a crisp crust around the edge that comes clean away from the sides of the mould as it cooks, allowing the soufflé to rise to unprecedented heights. This method was developed by David Chambers at Le Meridien, and it is foolproof, effectively turning the sides of the mould into a skid ring, to which nothing can adhere. The soufflé cannot tear or topple and the result is a textbook picture: a perfect, glossy flat surface, several inches above the rim of the dish.

A layer of finely chopped watercress and a hint of celery line the base of the soufflé. Eat this on its own, or accompany with bread.

To line mould

4oz/115g unsalted butter, clarified	2oz/55g freshly grated Parmesan

Watercress layer

1 stick celery	1/20z/15g unsalted butter
4oz/115g watercress (trimmed weight)	salt, pepper

Soufflé

2oz/55g unsalted butter	salt, pepper
2oz/55g plain flour	freshly grated nutmeg
10fl oz/275ml milk	4 egg yolks (size 2)
6oz/170g mature Cheddar, grated	7 egg whites (size 2)

To line the mould, swill the inside of an 8 inch/20cm soufflé dish with half the clarified butter. Dust this with half the Parmesan cheese and chill the dish until it sets. Repeat the process with the remaining butter and Parmesan, tipping out the excess cheese, and chill the dish again.

Finely chop the celery and peel the stalk, unless it is from the celery heart. Finely chop the watercress. Heat the ¹/₂oz/15g of butter in a frying pan and sweat the celery for a couple of minutes. Add the watercress and cook a couple of minutes longer, then season.

To make the soufflé, melt the butter in a small saucepan, stir in the flour and cook the roux for a couple of minutes. Take off the heat and gradually incorporate the milk, then cook the sauce for 4 minutes, stirring. Stir in the grated cheese and season with salt, pepper and nutmeg. Remove the pan from the heat, allow the sauce to cool for a minute or two and then add the egg yolks.

Preheat the oven to 200°C/400°F/Gas 6. Whisk the egg whites until stiff, stir a couple of spoons into the sauce and then incorporate the remainder as deftly as possible. Spread the watercress over the base of the soufflé dish. Pour the soufflé mixture over and place immediately in the oven, giving it plenty of headroom. Turn the oven down to 160°C/325°F/Gas 2 after 5 minutes. Do not open the door for the first 20 minutes. The soufflé will take 25-30 minutes to cook; ideally it will be *baveuse* in the centre, so act on the side of caution.

Huevos Revueltos

In Spain a poached egg may be added to a dish of slowly braised vegetables such as artichokes and broad beans, or piperade, slipped into the pot just before the end of cooking. An egg dish which appears on the menu of almost every tapas bar and restaurant is revueltos. A revueltos is like a scrambled omelette; the content may vary to include broad beans, mushrooms, peppers, peas, artichokes, asparagus and thin strips of ham, all of which are added in high proportion to the eggs, unlike a traditional omelette which is mainly egg with a modicum of filling. Like the best egg dishes, the revueltos is versatile, and may be as humble as a quick lunch using up odds and ends, or made into an exotic dish with asparagus, peas and morels. I ate a particularly memorable one in Seville, made with wild mushrooms and truffles.

This recipe feeds 2 people and is made in a 10 inch/25cm frying pan. If increasing the quantity, make in two lots or a larger pan.

---

1 small red pepper
2 tablespoons extra virgin olive oil
1 garlic clove, minced
6oz/170g asparagus, cooked

3oz/85g peas, cooked
salt, pepper
6 eggs (size 2)

Peel, core and deseed the pepper, and cut it into strips. Heat 1 tablespoon of olive oil in a frying pan and cook the pepper and garlic for a few minutes until limp and tender. Add the asparagus and peas to heat through, and season. While this mixture can be prepared in advance, it should be reheated before it is mixed with the eggs: the brief cooking time of the next stage is insufficient for it to heat thoroughly.

Whisk the eggs in a bowl, season, and combine with the vegetables. Heat the remaining olive oil in the frying pan over a high heat; when it smokes tip out the excess. Pour in the egg mixture and scramble with a fork. It will cook in about 30 seconds. Pile on to a plate while it is still slightly moist.

Chakchouka with Harissa and Mint

A chakchouka is a popular north African dish. Its makeup can vary, and each book I consult gives a slightly different definition. The dish consists of a base of braised vegetables similar to a ratatouille, which can include onions, peppers, tomatoes, courgettes, aubergines, artichokes, carrots, potatoes, green beans, peas, broad beans and cauliflower. Sometimes it is lightly spiced and can contain 'Mergues', a hot, spicy sausage. Unusual aspects of this dish are the flavouring of caraway, the harissa and the chopped mint scattered over at the very end.

Most chakchoukas include eggs, which are broken over the surface or mixed in with it and cooked until they set. It is highly versatile, substantial and easy to make and I would classify it as comfort food.

1 small onion	1 heaped tablespoon tomato purée
1 large carrot	1 scant teaspoon harissa
1/2 small cauliflower	1/2 teaspoon ground caraway
1 red pepper	salt
3oz/85g green beans	1/2 pint/300ml water
1 aubergine	3oz/85g peas
3 tablespoons extra virgin olive oil	6 eggs (size 2)
1 potato	1 dessertspoon chopped mint

Peel and chop the onion. Peel the carrot, halve it lengthwise and slice thickly. Cut the cauliflower into small florets. Remove the core and seeds from the pepper, halve and slice it. Top and tail the beans and cut them in half. Cut the aubergine into 1/2 inch/1cm cubes. Heat half the oil in a large saucepan and cook the aubergine for a couple of minutes until it just starts to colour; reserve it in a bowl. Heat the remaining oil and cook the rest of the prepared vegetables for 3 minutes. Peel and cube the potato; add this and the aubergine to the pan.

Blend the tomato purée, harissa, caraway and salt with ¹/₂ pint/300ml of water, pour this over the vegetables, bring to the boil and simmer, covered, for 15 minutes. Add the peas and cook without the lid until the vegetables are coated in a thickened sauce, which will take around 5-7 minutes. Check the salt.

Break the eggs over the stew, dispensing with one of the whites (or leave it if you happen to be partial to whites). Replace the saucepan lid and cook for a further 4-6 minutes until the yolks are set on the outside. Sprinkle over the chopped mint and serve.

Scrambled Eggs with Saffron and Shiitake Mushrooms

During medieval times when it was fashionable to colour food in dramatic tones, saffron was added to eggs as a matter of course to make them more yellow.

Because this is such a straightforward dish it does require the interest of some good mushrooms. The common-or-garden basic cultivated types will not be flavoursome enough. Shiitake will do, otherwise throw some wild mushrooms in with some cultivated ones.

Toast

4 thin slices white bread	*1¹/₂oz/45g unsalted butter, clarified*

Eggs

12 saffron filaments	*12 eggs (size 2)*
4 tablespoons double cream	*salt, pepper*

Mushrooms

1lb/450g shiitake mushrooms	*1 tablespoon flat-leaf parsley,*
1¹/₂oz/45g unsalted butter	*finely chopped*

To prepare the toast, heat the oven to 180°C/350°F/Gas 4. Remove the crusts from the bread and cut into triangles. Lay these on a baking sheet and cook for 4-5 minutes until they have dried out. Paint each side with the melted butter and return to the oven for 10-12 minutes until crisp and golden. Allow to cool on parchment paper or a rack before stacking.

Toast the saffron in a dry frying pan for 1 minute and grind it. Heat a tablespoon of the cream and infuse the saffron for 10 minutes. Whisk the eggs and pass through a sieve, then add the remaining cream, the saffron cream and seasoning. Wipe the mushrooms and slice.

You need to cook the mushrooms and eggs at the same time. Heat half the butter in a frying pan and when the foam subsides cover the base with mushrooms. Cook for about 4 minutes until soft, then cook the remainder of the mushrooms in the same way. Season, and stir in the parsley.

Heat the eggs in a small saucepan over a medium heat, stirring constantly with a wooden spoon to make sure they do not stick to the bottom of the pan. Stop cooking while they are on the moist side.

Pile the eggs on to plates, with the mushrooms on top and toast around.

Scrambled Eggs with Asparagus and Pistachio Butter

Asparagus and pistachio butter is delicious even without the eggs, but together they make a particularly appealing dish. You may want to serve toast as well.

2oz/55g pistachios	*12oz/340g asparagus sprue*
2oz/55g unsalted butter	*1 x scrambled eggs as above,*
salt, cayenne pepper	*omitting saffron*

Grind the pistachios in an electric grinder, blend with the butter using a wooden spoon, and season with salt and cayenne pepper. Chill until required.

Trim the asparagus where it becomes pale and tough, and peel each spear to within a couple of inches of the tip. Cook these at the same time as scrambling the eggs; the time they take to cook will depend on the thickness of the spears, approximately 4 minutes. Cook them in boiling salted water and season with salt when they are drained.

Melt the pistachio butter, which will become a thick paste, and toss the asparagus with it so it becomes thoroughly coated. Divide the scrambled eggs between the plates and place some spears on top.

Chinese Scrambled Eggs with Chives

This recipe employs a wok to scramble the eggs, which cook to light flakes streaked with the green of the chives. It is quite different to the creamy scrambled eggs traditional to Britain. Serve this dish with the toast described in the recipe for scrambled eggs with saffron and shiitake mushrooms (page 68). This recipe is based on one in Yan-Kit's *Classic Chinese Cookbook*.

---

10 eggs (size 2)	*7 tablespoons arachide oil*
salt, pepper	*2oz/55g chives*

Whisk the eggs, pass through a sieve, season and add 2 tablespoons of the oil. Trim the chives and cut into lengths 1$\frac{1}{2}$ inches/4cm long.

'Heat a wok over a high heat until smoke rises. Add the remaining oil, swirl it around and heat until very hot. Add the chives, stir for about 20 seconds, then pour in the egg. Sliding the wok scoop or metal spatula to the bottom of the wok, keep turning and letting the egg go under to blend with the oil and chives. Continue this way until all the egg has just set.'

Remove from the heat while you scoop the egg and chives mixture on to a warm serving plate. Serve immediately.

Salad 'Gribiche'

This is a strongly flavoured salad: rocket, radishes and olives balance the capers, gherkins and onion in the dressing. Finely minced egg yolk and white crown the top.

Dressing

2 tablespoons gherkins	¹/₂ teaspoon Dijon mustard
2 tablespoons capers	8 tablespoons extra virgin olive oil
1 dessertspoon balsamic vinegar	¹/₄ red onion, finely chopped
salt, pepper	

Croûtons

3 slices white bread, ¹/₂ inch/1cm thick	olive oil

Salad

4 eggs (size 2)	4oz/115g mangetouts
¹/₂ oak-leaf lettuce	2oz/55g radishes
few leaves of radicchio	3oz/85g olives, pitted
¹/₂oz/15g lamb's lettuce	1 punnet mustard and cress
¹/₂oz/15g rocket	

Rinse the gherkins and capers and chop. Whisk the balsamic vinegar with salt, pepper and the mustard. Add the olive oil and remaining ingredients for the dressing.

Cut the crusts off the bread and cut into cubes. Heat a few millimetres of olive oil in a frying pan and fry the croûtons until golden and crisp, turning them constantly. Drain on kitchen paper.

Hard-boil the eggs for 10 minutes. Cool them in cold water, shell them and separate the yolks from the whites. Mince the yolks and an equal quantity of egg white.

Discard the outer tough leaves of the oak-leaf lettuce and just use the leaf part of the remainder, discarding the stalk. Cut off and reserve the red leaf part of the radicchio, discarding the tough white part. Twist the roots from the lamb's lettuce. Wash these leaves with the rocket and place in a large bowl.

Top and tail the mangetouts and cut into long, thin strips. Blanch them for 20 seconds, cool them in cold water, drain and reserve. Slice the radishes. Toss the mangetouts, radishes, croûtons and olives into the leaves. Toss this with the dressing. Place clumps of cress here and there. Finally place the minced egg yolk in the centre and the white around this.

Frittata with Herbs and Summer Vegetables

This is a deep omelette, baked in the oven. The eggs are broken but not whisked, so the surface is streaked with yellow and white and the red of the pepper shows through.

6oz/170g broad beans	*6 eggs (size 2)*
6oz/170g courgettes	*5fl oz/150ml double cream*
1 onion	*2 tablespoons freshly grated*
1 red pepper	*Parmesan*
1 tablespoon extra virgin olive oil	*salt, pepper*

Finely chopped herbs

1 level tablespoon each of flat-leaf parsley, chives, dill, marjoram	*1 heaped teaspoon tarragon*

Steam the broad beans for 5 minutes, and skin them once cool. Quarter the courgettes lengthwise and slice ¼ inch/0.25cm thick, steam for 2 minutes and reserve. Peel and chop the onion, remove the core and seeds from the pepper and dice. Heat the olive oil in a frying pan and cook the onion and pepper for 10 minutes over a medium-low heat until soft but not coloured. Combine all the vegetables in a bowl and season.

Preheat the oven to 200°C/400°F/Gas 6. Crack the eggs into a bowl and add the cream, Parmesan, seasoning and herbs. Break the yolks but do not whisk. Gently fold the vegetables into this, just folding over once or twice. Pour into a greased 10 inch/25cm frying pan with heatproof handle or a similar-sized gratin dish, and bake in the oven for approximately 20 minutes, until the omelette is firm and golden.

Welsh Rarebit

The history of Welsh Rabbit, or Rarebit as it later became known, goes back as far as the early eighteenth century. It must be one of the few English foods adopted by the French: 'le welsh' became a popular item on the menu of turn-of-the-century French restaurants, washed down by pewter tankards of ale.

The Esquire Party Book, an American guide to entertaining published in 1935, is an extraordinary testament to American lifestyle at that time. Perhaps unfairly it indicates that drink-around-the-clock was quite the norm, and it is fair to assume that everyone must have had livers of steel. Liquid suggestions for breakfast include Screwdrivers, Hot Buttered Rum, Dubonnet, the Blood Shot and a Connecticut Bullfrog; or 'More A.M. Brighteners' such as a Savannah, Honolulu, Golden Glow, Pale Deacon or Nevada. Also Hangover Cures likely to render you unconscious if they don't do the trick. At lunchtime you could look forward to a Churchill Cocktail, a Frozen Daiquiri, a Mint Julep or a Rob Roy, and on to Tea, the 'Cocktail Hour' and Dinner and so to bed. A recipe for Welsh Rabbit is given as a 'spur-of-the-moment snack for the hours after midnight', at which point it must assume magical absorption qualities.

There does not seem to be any one authentic version; rather there are many versions, some given over to other flavourings, or to other countries – 'American', 'Scotch' and so forth. This recipe amalgamates elements I feel to be essential: a drop of stout, some mustard, a touch of heat from the Tabasco, and egg which binds the mixture and gives it its consistency. Many of the recipes I tried quoted absurd amounts of ale, stout or wine which reduced the cheese mixture to a thin custard. The method below, where the ingredients for the topping are blended, then spread on the toast and grilled, allows you to pile the cheese more thickly on the toast than if you blended the ingredients over a low heat and poured the sauce over.

Cocktail-size rarebits can be prepared as an hors d'oeuvre. Cut the toast small, then place some cheese on each piece and grill it.

9oz/250g mature Cheddar cheese, grated	*2fl oz/55ml stout*
	1 teaspoon Worcestershire sauce
1oz/30g unsalted butter	*few drops Tabasco*
2 tablespoons breadcrumbs	*black pepper*
1 egg (size 2), beaten	*4 large or 6 medium slices day-old*
1 level teaspoon Dijon mustard	*bread, crusts removed*

Using a wooden spoon, blend the cheese and butter in a bowl, then incorporate the remaining ingredients, except the bread. Cover and chill for several hours until very firm.

Toast the bread and spread each slice of toast thickly with the cheese mixture. Grill under a medium to low grill for 5 minutes in order to cook the inside of the mixture, then turn the grill up high to brown the top.

Cheese Fondue

Fondues were a seventies phenomenon which seemed to disappear along with glam rock, Mary Quant and her daisies, and the colour orange. I remember the seventies as a time when every colour supplement would carry a special offer for a fondue set, and many was the Saturday morning I earned my pocket money polishing one of these things. This craze was more about 'fondue bourguignonne', a particularly unpleasant ritual of dipping pieces of raw meat into hot oil and, once cooked, into a number of sauces. It seems this trend has served to sully the reputation of all fondues, a Swiss cheese fondue included. Cheese fondue is quite delicious and embarrassingly simple to prepare: it takes about 5 minutes to cook. This fondue automatically counts as party fodder because it is a centrepiece, and the nature of eating it is communal. It is very rich and very substantial and calls for a cautious choice of dishes either side. With all the speciality breads in the shops it has never been more timely. Choose a selection of breads: German rye, a crusty country-style white bread, and some breads flavoured with walnut, herbs or garlic.

Traditionally a cheese fondue is made in an earthenware or thick enamel dish with a handle, called a *caquelon*, which is kept hot over a spirit burner; and special long forks can be bought. Do not be deterred if you do not have these items. Use your best saucepan – Le Creuset and that type are fine, otherwise use a heavy stainless steel one. Decant the fondue into a hot dish, and in the absence of a burner appoint a stirrer; the fondue will retain its heat for about 15 minutes. If you start to run into trouble and the cheese begins to set, then simply reheat it.

It goes without saying that attention must be paid to the quality of the cheeses and the wine. Buy cheese cut from a whole rather than plastic wrapped; as to the wine, an oaky Chardonnay is appropriate. I have added some of the wine and kirsch at the end to add some of the raw flavour of these liquids back to the fondue, otherwise all their character is boiled away as the fondue is prepared.

14oz/400g bread with crust	*1 dessertspoon cornflour*
10oz/285g Gruyère	*1 tablespoon kirsch, plus*
10oz/285g Emmenthal	*1 dessertspoon*
1 garlic clove	*freshly grated nutmeg*
12fl oz/325ml white wine	*salt, pepper*

Cut the bread into 1 inch/2cm cubes and set aside. Thinly slice both cheeses and reserve separately. Crush the clove of garlic to a paste and spread it on the base of the fondue pot, then scrape most of it off and discard; this will give a good concentration of garlic without being too strong. I find the practice of rubbing the inside of a bowl with a whole clove of garlic to be rather pointless, because the flavour afforded to the dish is more or less imperceptible.

Pour 10fl oz/275ml of the white wine into the pan and heat to a simmer. Add the Emmenthal and cook over a high heat, stirring vigorously, until it is melted and boiling. Mix the cornflour with the tablespoon of kirsch, add to the pan, turn the heat down low and stir the fondue until it stabilizes into a homogeneous sauce. Add the Gruyère and continue to stir until it is melted and incorporated into the fondue. Season with freshly grated nutmeg, salt and pepper. Stir in the remaining wine and kirsch and serve as soon as it is smooth. It is customary for diners to stand while the lid of the fondue is removed.

Glamorgan Sausages

Traditionally the bulk of these sausages consists of breadcrumbs, but they are lighter and more delicate made with quinoa, which is available in health food stores and some supermarkets. Serve with the celeriac purée on page 181.

5oz/140g quinoa	*1 spring onion, finely chopped*
6oz/170g Provolone or Pecorino	*salt, pepper*
2 heaped tablespoons parsley,	*2 egg yolks (size 2)*
finely chopped	*2 eggs (size 2), beaten*
1 level teaspoon thyme, finely	*fine breadcrumbs*
chopped	*vegetable oil for deep-frying*
1/2 teaspoon sage, finely chopped	

Bring a pan of salted water to the boil and cook the quinoa for 15 minutes. Drain and run cold water through it, then reserve.

Grate the cheese, mix this with the quinoa and add the herbs, onion and seasoning. Whisk the egg yolks and blend them into the mixture.

Make cylindrical sausages 3 inches/8cm in length and 1 inch/2cm in diameter; a certain dexterity and degree of optimism are necessary at this stage, but they will hold together with care. Place them on a plate or Tupperware lid and chill them for 1 hour, which will firm them. Coat the sausages first in the beaten egg and then in the breadcrumbs and chill for 30 minutes. They will keep like this in the fridge overnight.

Heat the oil so it is medium-hot but not smoking, and deep-fry the sausages until they are golden all over – this takes only 4-5 minutes. Drain them on kitchen paper and serve with the celeriac purée.

Baked Goat's Cheese with Roasted Garlic, and Focaccia with Coriander and Rocket

I love this particular assembly, which is very satisfying to eat: squeezing the softly baked garlic cloves from their casing, dipping the warm bread with its oily, golden crust into the thyme-scented oil, then piling it with the hot goat's cheese, which is mousse-like in consistency.

Goat's cheeses come in varying sizes, so choose one small one per person or the equivalent in larger ones. Select a semi-matured, or demi-sec cheese, though the small mature cheeses will also bake well. The most famous French cheese used for such baking is Crottin de Chavignol. The Spanish *queso de cabra*, marinated in olive oil and herbs, and a range of British imitations, especially the Innes goat's cheeses, will also bake well. To date I have not found a suitable cheese in a supermarket, so try to buy from a specialized outlet and if in doubt ask for advice. The goat's cheeses can also be spread with a little minced garlic and chopped tarragon or oregano.

The focaccia is based on the recipe for pizza dough on page 109.

Focaccia

$^1/_2$ *teaspoon dried yeast or*
 $^1/_2$*oz/15g fresh yeast*
$^1/_2$ *teaspoon caster sugar*
$10^1/_2$*oz/300g strong white flour*
1 *heaped teaspoon salt*
4 *tablespoons olive oil*

approx. 6fl oz/175ml hand-hot
 water
1 *teaspoon coriander seeds*
fine-grain sea salt, pepper
$^3/_4$*oz/20g rocket*

If using fresh yeast, dissolve it in a little of the water, adding the sugar, and leave it for 10 minutes until a froth appears on the surface. Add this to the dry ingredients and proceed as if using dried yeast.

Place all the dry ingredients in a bowl, add 1 tablespoon of olive oil and gradually add the water, bringing the dough together with your hand. The amount of water is for guidance only. If you add too much, simply sprinkle on some more flour until you have a workable dough again. Knead the dough on a floured surface until it is smooth and elastic – this will take around 8-10 minutes. This operation can be performed in an orbital mixer, and some food processors do a fairly good job, in which case halve the kneading time.

Place the dough in a bowl brushed with oil, slash a cross on the surface to facilitate its rising, and sprinkle on a little more flour. Loosely cover with a plastic bag and place in a warm, draught-free spot. Leave it to rise for between 1 and 3 hours until it has doubled in volume. I favour a long slow rising, which gives a better flavour.

Punch the dough down, sprinkling it with flour as necessary, and knead it for a minute or two. Roll the dough into a round cake about $1/2$ inch/1cm thick and 8-9 inches/20-22cm in diameter, and place it on an oiled baking sheet. Cover it loosely with a plastic bag and leave to rise until double in volume, about 1-2 hours.

Preheat the oven to its highest setting. Coarsely crush the coriander seeds. Indent the surface of the focaccia with your thumb and trickle over 1 tablespoon of olive oil. Sprinkle over some fine-grain sea salt, a grinding of black pepper and the coriander seeds. Cook the focaccia for 20 minutes. Tear the rocket into pieces and toss with 2 tablespoons of olive oil, scatter over the surface of the focaccia and cook for another 5 minutes until the rocket is crisp but still green, and the focaccia below is uniformly golden. Serve it in large pieces when it has cooled for a few minutes.

Roasted garlic

5 heads garlic (or 1 per person)	4 tablespoons extra virgin olive oil
5 sprigs thyme	1oz/30g unsalted butter
salt, pepper	

Goat's cheeses

goat's cheeses	extra virgin olive oil

While the focaccia is rising for the second time, bake the garlic. Preheat the oven to 140°C/275°F/Gas 1. Cut the top off each head of garlic to reveal the cloves and place in a shallow baking dish. Tuck the sprigs of thyme in here and there, season well, pour over the olive oil and dot with the butter. Cover with foil and cook for 1¼ hours, basting every so often. Serve warm, but not so it is too hot to handle.

Lastly bake the goat's cheese, which takes only 10 minutes. Place them in a shallow ovenproof dish, trickle a little olive oil over the cheese, and cook in a hot oven for 10 minutes, until it turns a honeyed gold in patches. The cheese should retain its shape, while being molten inside.

Gougère served with Green Peppers in a Tomato Sauce with Cumin

Produce a gougère around drinks time and observe as it steadily reduces in circumference. Use a decent mature Cheddar.

3oz/85g unsalted butter	*6¹/₂oz/185g Cheddar, grated*
11fl oz/300ml water	*1oz/30g Parmesan*
pinch salt	*black pepper*
6oz/170g plain flour, sieved	*pinch freshly grated nutmeg*
5 eggs (size 2)	

Melt the butter together with the water and salt in a saucepan. When the mixture boils remove it from the heat and beat in the flour. Return the pan to the heat and cook the dough for a couple of minutes. Remove the pan from the heat, allow it to cool slightly, then beat in the eggs one at a time. The dough should remain stiff. Stir in the cheeses, reserving 2oz/55g of the Cheddar; season with pepper and nutmeg.

Preheat the oven to 180°C/350°F/Gas 4. Butter and flour 2 large baking sheets. Place heaped teaspoons of the dough, just touching, in a circle on each tray (approx 8 inches/20cm). Smooth the domes with a teaspoon, dipping it into water as you work. Scatter the remaining cheese over the crests of the spheres and bake for 35-45 minutes until quite a deep gold. To prevent choux pastry from turning soft it should be pierced in places immediately it comes out of the oven; this allows the steam to escape. It is best eaten while it is warm.

Green Peppers in a Tomato Sauce with Cumin

A Sevillian summer is hot beyond imagination. Electric fans actually serve to make you hotter, circulating air the temperature of a hair-drier. At times of the day the only solution is to sit with your feet in a bucket of cold water, changing it each time it warms up, simultaneously mopping your brow. It is small surprise that Sevillians desert their city at weekends, crowding out the beaches an hour or two's drive away. Following suit one weekend we thought we were quite clever to discover a nearly deserted beach. Deserted for a good reason since it was plagued by the Levante, a fierce wind which whipped the sand into a gritty storm. Sheltering in a beachside bar we ate lunch, which proved to be one of the best meals I ate in Spain. We had this dish of peppers flavoured with cumin, and a divine fish soup of tiny clams and vermicelli, flavoured with turmeric. With the mountains of Africa visible across the sea like some Moorish ghost, the subtle spicing came as a reminder of the role the Moors played in shaping Spanish food.

The peppers can also be cooked in the oven according to the instructions on page 9, but will not have the same smoky flavour.

---

3 green peppers	$^1/_3$ teaspoon caster sugar
4 marmande tomatoes	salt, pepper
1 garlic clove	$^3/_4$ teaspoon cumin seeds
6 tablespoons extra virgin olive oil	juice of $^1/_2$ lemon
1 dessertspoon tomato purée	$^1/_4$ red onion

Heat a griddle and cook the peppers on all sides until they are charred and the skin is blistering. Place them inside two plastic bags, one inside the other, secure the bags and leave the peppers to steam as they cool. Remove the skin and seeds, reserving any juices given out, and cut into strips.

Skin, seed and slice the tomatoes, and mince the garlic. Heat half the olive oil in a medium-sized saucepan, add the garlic, and when it gives off its aroma add the tomatoes, tomato purée, sugar and seasoning, and cook until this reduces to quite a thick sauce, for about 10 minutes. Add the peppers and cook a further 5 minutes, remove to a shallow dish and cool to room temperature.

Toast the cumin for a couple of minutes in a dry frying pan and grind it with a pestle and mortar. Stir this into the peppers, then add the lemon juice, remaining olive oil and reserved pepper juices; adjust seasoning. To serve, cut the onion into thin slivers and scatter over the peppers. Serve this with the gougère.

Gratin of Celery with Lovage and Truffle Oil, served with Parmesan and Chilli Muffins

Along with the bottles on my drinks tray sits a curiosity called 'Old English Lovage Alcoholic Cordial', which recommends mixing it with 2 parts brandy to 'really set you up'. It remains full to the brim after several years of standing there, which is small recommendation for such a delicious herb. To date I have not found lovage for sale, but it grows well, in fact up to a stupendous eight feet tall, and if you have a garden it is a worthy bush. Use only the young and tender green leaves, and if no lovage is to be had use 2 tablespoons of the celery foliage.

Anyone who has had one too many memorably bad white sauces has reason to hate them, but if well made and used correctly they can be delicious. It is essential when stringing the celery to be thorough with the outside sticks, and discard the toughest-looking pieces.

---

2 heads of celery
2 carrots, peeled
1 onion, peeled
sprig of thyme, bay leaf, parsley
  stalk
salt, pepper
2oz/55g unsalted butter
1¹/₂oz/45g plain flour

6fl oz/175ml milk
6fl oz/175ml double cream
7fl oz/200ml reduced stock
  (see below)
2 level dessertspoons lovage, finely
  chopped
2 teaspoons truffle oil

Preheat the oven to 180°C/350°F/Gas 4. Trim the celery, string each stalk with a potato peeler, wash it and cut into 4 inch/10cm lengths. Coarsely chop the carrots and onion and place together with the herbs in a casserole. Place the celery on top, half cover with water, and season. Cover with foil and fit with a lid. Place in the oven and cook for 1 hour. Remove the celery to a gratin dish so the sticks lie in the same direction. Transfer the contents of the casserole, including the carrot and onion, to a saucepan and reduce the liquid to approximately 7fl oz/200ml; strain and reserve it. Turn the oven up to 200°C/400°F/Gas 6. Melt the butter in a saucepan, stir in the flour and cook the roux for a couple of minutes. Gradually incorporate the milk, the cream and the reduced stock, season and cook for 5 minutes, stirring it as necessary. Add the lovage and the truffle oil. Pour the sauce over the celery, mixing it down into it, and bake for 30 minutes until-patched with gold and bubbling at the edges. Accompany with the Parmesan and chilli muffins.

Parmesan and Chilli Muffins

Makes 16

The moulds should be thoroughly greased, as the muffins have a tendency to stick because of the Parmesan; alternatively use paper cups.

3oz/85g maize flour or meal	*³/₄ teaspoon chilli, minced*
5oz/140g plain flour	*4oz/115g unsalted butter*
2 teaspoons baking powder	*2 eggs (size 2)*
¹/₄ teaspoon salt	*7fl oz/200ml milk*
2¹/₂oz/70g freshly grated Parmesan	

Heat the oven to 200°C/400°F/Gas 6 and butter the muffin moulds, which should have steep sides and a flat base. Sieve together the flours and baking powder and add the salt, Parmesan and chilli. Beat the butter in a food processor until pale and creamy. Beat the eggs into the butter then remove to a bowl. Very gently work half the dry ingredients and half the milk into the butter and egg mixture, then the other half – do not overwork it, the batter will still be lumpy. Spoon the batter into the muffin moulds so they are two-thirds full, and bake for 17-20 minutes. Loosen with a knife and turn on to a wire rack to cool for 10 minutes.

Ploughman's with a Sweet Tomato and Sesame Chutney

The star of this assembly is the chutney, which started life as an accompaniment to barbecued duck breasts in a *Vogue* feature on sauces. It is sumptuous, crimson and aromatic, studded with sesame seeds and raisins. Take fresh white rolls, slit and butter them, on the lower half place some slices of a good Cheddar cheese, a generous dollop of this chutney and some thin slivers of spring onion, close the rolls and eat.

Cheese and chutney is peculiarly eccentric and British, obviously left over from the days of the Raj when Indian customs in food were borrowed and moulded to suit the British palate. In fact up until the 1950s or 60s an anglicized Indian woman, or an Anglo-Indian, was referred to by conservative Indians as a 'Chutney Mary'. Hence the restaurant of the same name in the King's Road, London; the food served here is a blend of British and Indian.

Sweet Tomato and Sesame Chutney

8fl oz/225ml champagne vinegar,
  or white wine vinegar
6oz/170g caster sugar
1lb/450g marmande tomatoes,
  skinned and chopped
1/8 teaspoon fennel seeds, ground
pinch each of mace, garam masala,
  cayenne pepper, powdered ginger

4 cardamom pods, cracked
1 bay leaf
3/4 teaspoon salt
1/2 oz raisins
1 heaped dessertspoon white
  sesame seeds

Heat the vinegar and sugar together until it melts, then add the tomatoes, all the spices, the bay leaf and the salt. Cook this at a steady boil for 25 minutes, then remove the bay leaf and cardamom pods. Add the raisins and sesame seeds and cook over a low heat for another 8 minutes, stirring regularly. The chutney will set to a jam-like consistency on cooling and should keep for a couple of weeks in the refrigerator.

See also:

Mushrooms

Mushroom Names

When it comes to mushroom names, I think it is fair to say the French have succeeded in complicating things in the case of chanterelles and girolles. To avoid any confusion, mushrooms referred to in this section as girolles are *Cantharellus cibarius* and those referred to as chanterelles are *Cantharellus tubaeformis*. If elsewhere you find chanterelles referred to as either grey, brown or yellow, then you had best consult a Frenchman! It is also worth mentioning that what the French call girolles are also called chanterelles.

Porcini Salad

Porcini are one of the few wild mushrooms that are good eaten raw. You will require small ones, about 2½ inches/6cm tall, and a mixture of extra virgin olive oil and arachide oil, or a very mild extra virgin olive oil, so as not to overwhelm the delicate flavour of the porcini.

12oz/340g fresh porcini	*salt, pepper*
3 tablespoons extra virgin olive oil	*1 dessertspoon flat-leaf parsley,*
3 tablespoons arachide oil	*finely chopped*

Scrape the porcini clean with a knife. Shortly before serving the salad, slice them very thinly – a mandolin will help. Gently to avoid breaking the slices, toss them with the oils, seasoning and parsley and serve straight away.

Warm Salad of Girolles with Rocket, Baby Spinach and a Mustard Mayonnaise

Girolles are one of the most prized of the wild mushrooms, heady with the scent of apricots. Here their juice is combined with a mustard mayonnaise to produce a thin sauce, trickled over the hot mushrooms and leaves underneath. The amount of water a mushroom will contain can vary, and sometimes almost no juices are given off. If this is the case, deglaze the pan with 2fl oz/55ml white wine, letting it cook a minute or two, then stir it into the mayonnaise. Alternatively soak a few dried mushrooms in boiling water and use a little of the soaking water. I ate a version of this salad at a small trattoria in Trento, Northern Italy. It was the first course of a lengthy menu of mushroom dishes.

Only half the mayonnaise will be required for this recipe, but it would be difficult to make a smaller quantity.

Mustard mayonnaise

1 egg yolk (size 2)	5fl oz/150ml arachide oil
1 teaspoon Dijon mustard	salt

3oz/85g baby spinach, washed	1 garlic clove, minced
1/2oz/15g rocket, washed	1 heaped teaspoon flat-leaf
14oz/400g girolles (see page 95)	parsley, finely chopped
1 1/2oz/45g unsalted butter,	salt, pepper
clarified	1 tablespoon extra virgin olive oil

Make a mayonnaise by whisking the egg yolk with the mustard, then slowly whisking in the oil. Season with salt and reserve half for use in another recipe.

Slice the baby spinach and rocket into broad strips and place in a bowl. Scrape and trim the mushrooms and slice if they are large. Cook the mushrooms in two lots so as not to overcrowd the pan. Heat some butter in a frying pan and throw in the mushrooms together with the garlic, parsley and seasoning. Cook over a gentle heat until the juices are running, then remove to a bowl. Stir the mushroom juices into the mustard mayonnaise. Now fry the mushrooms a second time in a little more butter. If as mentioned above the mushrooms do not give out any juices, then only fry them once.

To serve the salad, toss the leaves with olive oil, season, and place on individual plates or a large platter. Arrange the mushrooms on top of the leaves, trickle mustard mayonnaise over and serve immediately.

Potato Gratin with Wild Mushrooms and Fontina

I love this gratin, it is homely and uncomplicated. The potatoes cook in a cream richly fragrant with the mushrooms and there is nothing to upstage their flavour. Use any selection of wild mushrooms.

12oz/340g wild mushrooms	*5oz/140g Fontina cheese*
2oz/55g unsalted butter, clarified	*3fl oz/85ml double cream*
salt, pepper	*2fl oz/55ml white wine*
2lb/900g potatoes	*2fl oz/55ml vegetable stock*

Pick over the mushrooms and chop them coarsely. Heat half the butter in a frying pan and when it is very hot throw in half the mushrooms so that they all hit the oil at once. If you cook them in this fashion they will sear, and any liquid given out should vaporize; a cooler fat allows the liquid to be drawn out and they end up stewing. Cook for approximately 2 minutes, then remove to a bowl and cook the other half of the mushrooms in the remaining butter. Season them. Peel and slice the potatoes very thinly, discarding the end slice.

Preheat the oven to 190°C/375°F/Gas 5. Slice the Fontina cheese. Combine the cream, wine and vegetable stock and season. Butter a gratin dish which will allow 3 layers of potato and 2 of mushrooms – I usually use an 8 inch/20cm casserole. Arrange a layer of potatoes on the base and season, then some mushrooms and Fontina cheese, and repeat these layers ending with a layer of potatoes. Pour the cream mixture over and bake for 1 hour.

Mushrooms à la Grècque with Herbs and Tomato

Button mushrooms are poached in an aromatic broth which is then reduced, some finely chopped fresh basil and coriander are added, and some tomato concassée is served with it – bread is essential.

Mushrooms

1 1/2lb/675g button mushrooms	12 black peppercorns
1/2 pint/300ml water	1/4 teaspoon fennel seeds
1/8 pint/75ml good extra virgin olive oil	6 coriander seeds
	1 shallot, finely chopped
juice of 1/2 lemon	6 parsley stalks
1/2 teaspoon salt	

Dressing

1 dessertspoon each of coriander, parsley, basil, finely chopped	lemon juice
	salt, pepper
3 tablespoons good extra virgin olive oil	1 marmande tomato, or 8oz/225g tomatoes

Wipe the mushrooms clean and trim the stalks if necessary. Make an aromatic broth by combining all the remaining ingredients for the mushrooms in a pan; contain the seeds in a small square of muslin. Bring the broth to the boil and simmer, covered, for 10 minutes.

Add the mushrooms, bring the broth back to the boil, cover the pan, turn the heat down low and simmer for 10 minutes, stirring once. Remove the mushrooms to a bowl and reduce the remaining broth to several tablespoons of liquid. Discard the seeds and strain the reduced liquor over the mushrooms. Allow them to cool. Stir in the herbs, add 2 tablespoons of the olive oil and sharpen with lemon juice if necessary, and adjust seasoning. Leave for 1 hour for the flavours of the herbs to permeate the dish.

Skin, deseed and dice the tomato, mix with the remaining tablespoon of olive oil and season with salt and pepper. Serve the mushrooms with a spoon of tomato in the centre.

Tagliatelle with Shiitake Mushrooms in a Cream Sauce

The fresh saffron tagliatelle on page 238 makes this a special pasta dish, but the ordinary shop-bought fresh pasta is quite adequate. This is a very simple and easy dish to prepare, as the sauce can be made in advance and reheated. Any characterful mushrooms or combination of mushrooms can be used; shiitake are now commonly available in large supermarkets. Dried wild mushrooms, reconstituted, are always a welcome addition; the liquid in which they have soaked can take the place of the vegetable stock in the recipe.

Mushroom sauce

3 shallots	*3fl oz/85ml vegetable stock*
1lb/450g shiitake mushrooms	*2 tablespoons freshly grated*
1oz/30g unsalted butter	*Parmesan*
3fl oz/85ml white wine	*salt, pepper*
6fl oz/175ml double cream	

12oz/340g fresh tagliatelle

Finely chop the shallots. Slice the mushrooms. Heat half the butter in a frying pan, add the shallots and cook them for a couple of minutes. Add half the mushrooms to the pan and cook for 3-4 minutes. Remove to a bowl and cook the remaining mushrooms in the same fashion. Return all the mushrooms to the pan, add the white wine and cook for a couple of minutes. Add the cream and vegetable stock and simmer the sauce for about 3 minutes until it thickens a little. Remove the pan from the heat and stir in the Parmesan and seasoning. Keep the sauce warm while the pasta cooks.

Bring a large pan of salted water to the boil and cook the pasta. Drain and toss it with the sauce, adjust the seasoning and serve.

Chanterelles Sauce with Tomato and Parsley

This sauce lends itself beautifully to pasta, polenta or potato gnocchi. Its roots lie in a recipe for a fricassée of wild mushrooms in *Cooking for Friends* by Raymond Blanc. The joy of cooking from such a book is that while the recipes appear to be lengthy, they are full of detailed intricacies which lead one to understand more about the science of cooking.

¹/₂₀z/15g dried porcini
¹/₄₀z/8g flat-leaf parsley leaves
1lb/450g chanterelles
  (see page 95)
3¹/₂₀z/100g unsalted butter
2 shallots, chopped
salt, pepper

lemon juice
1 tablespoon double cream
2 tomatoes, skinned, seeded
  and diced
1 heaped tablespoon chervil,
  finely chopped

Soak the porcini in 4fl oz/115ml boiling water for 15 minutes. Strain the liquor through a fine-mesh sieve and reserve it. Finely chop the porcini and reserve. Blanch the parsley leaves for 1-2 minutes or until they are tender. Strain and cool them in cold water and reserve.

Pick over the chanterelles to remove any pine needles and other plant matter – this is the most time-consuming part of this recipe. Use 1¹/₂₀z/45g of the butter to cook the mushrooms – heat ¹/₂₀z/15g at a time in a frying pan, add some of the chopped shallots, cook for 1 minute, then add some of the chanterelles and toss them, season with salt, pepper and a few drops of lemon, cover and cook them for 1 minute. Strain any juices into a small saucepan, reserve the chanterelles in a bowl and cook the remainder. Keep the mushrooms covered to keep them warm.

Add the chopped porcini to the chanterelles, and the soaking liquor to the chanterelles liquor. To make the sauce, heat this with the cream and whisk in the remaining butter. Add the tomato and parsley leaves to heat through, and the chervil. Season the sauce. If necessary briefly reheat the mushrooms. The chanterelles will have already collapsed since their juices have been extracted, but rough-handling will reduce them to a mush. Divide the mushrooms between the plates, then spoon the sauce over.

Artichoke Hearts with Wild Mushrooms and a Truffle Sabayon

I have prepared this dish using only horn of plenty mushrooms, which are excellent, but you can use any wild mushrooms. I have also made it with ordinary cultivated mushrooms and it is still good. Do not be put off by the 'truffle' in the sabayon, as it tastes just as good flavoured with lemon juice; nor by the word 'sabayon', for it is the simplest of sauces to prepare, basically a frothy hollandaise. This idea finds its origins at Gidleigh Park, where I watched Shaun Hill prepare a similar dish.

12oz/340g wild mushrooms	*salt, pepper*
5 large globe artichokes	*2oz/55g watercress fronds,*
1oz/30g unsalted butter	*2 inches/5cm in length*

Sabayon

6oz/170g unsalted butter	*salt*
2 egg yolks (size 2)	*truffle oil*
2fl oz/55ml white wine	

Clean the mushrooms carefully, slit them lengthwise if necessary to dislodge any insects that might have taken up residence, otherwise scrape them with a knife and slice if they are large. Pare and cook the artichokes according to the instructions on page 6, leaving the choke in place. Drain them and reserve in cold water; remove chokes and trim them when they are cool enough to handle.

Prepare the sabayon, which will keep for a couple of hours at room temperature. Heat the butter in a saucepan until it is molten and bubbling. Set a double boiler on the stove with $^1/_2$ inch/1cm of water in the bottom half. Whisk the egg yolks in the top half over a very low heat for 1-2 minutes, add the wine and continue whisking until you have a stable sabayon. Whisk in the melted butter gradually, transfer to a jug and season with salt and truffle oil.

Cook the mushrooms in batches to avoid overcrowding the pan. Melt a knob of butter in a frying pan and cook the mushrooms for 3 minutes. Remove them to a bowl and season with salt and pepper. Melt a little butter in the pan and wilt the watercress. Return the mushrooms to the pan to heat through.

Reheat the artichoke hearts either by steaming them, or plunging them into boiling water. Season them with salt. Place an artichoke heart on each plate, pile some mushrooms on top and spoon some sabayon over.

See also:
Scrambled Eggs with Saffron and Shiitake Mushrooms (page 68)
Mushrooms, Pecan Nuts and Beetroot on Sourdough Bread (page 127)
Orzotto ai Porcini (page 141)
Ravioli 'all U'ovo' with Wild Mushrooms (page 236)
Wild Mushroom Risotto (page 245)
Soft Polenta with Mixed Mushrooms and Fontina (page 259)

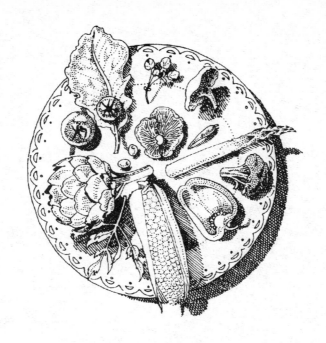

Pizza, Calzone and Sandwiches

Pizza Dough

Two recipes for pizza are included here: a pissaladière, or tomato and onion pizza with marjoram and olives, and an aubergine and goat's cheese pizza with roasted garlic. The pizza can be made as two 11 inch/27cm round pizzas, which will feed 3 people each; as 12 small individual pizzelle; or as an oblong pizza in a tray, in which case you will have some excess dough. Made in a tray and cut small they make simple hors d'oeuvre, and take a fraction of the time to prepare that miniature quiches do.

The recipe for the dough is taken from *Italian Pizza and Savoury Breads* by Elizabeth Romer.

$^{1}/_{2}$ teaspoon dried yeast or
* $^{1}/_{2}$oz/15g fresh yeast*
$^{1}/_{2}$ teaspoon caster sugar
$10^{1}/_{2}$oz/300g strong white flour

1 heaped teaspoon salt
1 tablespoon extra virgin olive oil
approx 6fl oz/175ml hand-hot
*   water*

If using fresh yeast, dissolve it in a little of the water, adding the sugar, and leave it for 10 minutes until a froth appears on the surface. Add this to the dry ingredients and proceed as if using dried yeast.

Place all the dry ingredients in a bowl, add the olive oil and gradually add the water, bringing the dough together with your hand. The amount of water is for guidance only. If you add too much, simply sprinkle on some more flour until you have a workable dough again. Knead the dough on a floured surface until it is smooth and elastic – this will take around 8-10 minutes. This operation can be performed in an orbital mixer, and some food processors do a fairly good job, but halve the kneading time.

Place the dough in a lightly floured bowl, slash a cross on the surface to facilitate its rising, and sprinkle on a little more flour. Loosely cover it with a plastic bag and place it in a warm, draught-free spot. Leave it to rise for between 1 and 3 hours until it has doubled in volume. I favour a long slow rising, which gives a better flavour.

Punch the dough down, sprinkling it with flour as necessary, and knead it for a minute or two. Flatten and roll the dough into the desired size. If using an oblong tray then partly roll and partly press the dough – it should be $^1/_8$ inch/0.25cm thick. Brush the dough with olive oil and dress it according to the recipe. When the pizza is cooked the edges will be thin and crisp; if you prefer a slightly spongier outside then rest the rolled pizza base for 20 minutes in a warm place before dressing it.

Perfectly good pizza can be made using standard baking trays. Aficionados of pizza and bread-making may well choose to use baking or quarry tiles, wooden paddles and so forth, but this is not really necessary for these recipes.

Pissaladière

This pizza is based on the regional speciality from Nice, pissaladière, though more accurately it should be called '*sardenaira*'. Elizabeth Romer says of this dish: 'All along the Ligurian coast of Italy stretching up and around to the French border then continuing along the southern coast of France, the local pizza is flavoured with onions. The name of the pizza changes at different points. In Italy it is known as sardenaira or pizzalandrea after the Italian Admiral Andrea Doria; further towards the French border it is called pizza di ventimiglia or pisciadela; in France itself, pissaladière. Until 1860 the coastal area up to and including Nice formed part of Italy and there are some Niçoise dishes that are closely tied to Italian, particularly Tuscan, recipes, both in name and ingredient.'

A regional speciality of Nice, pissaladière takes its name from *pissalat*, a condiment made from the fry of sardines and anchovies. Usually prepared in oblong trays, it is made from onions, herbs and *pissalat*, garnished with olives and anchovies. Shortcrust pastry can replace the bread dough as the base of the tart. The Italian *sardenaira*, native to the Ligurian coast, is basically the same with the addition of tomatoes.

---

1 *quantity of pizza dough*
  (see page 109)
2 *white onions*
1 *red onion*
3 *tablespoons olive oil*
1/2 *teaspoon thyme*
2 *garlic cloves*
2lb/900g *tomatoes, peeled, seeded*
  and chopped

1 *tablespoon tomato purée*
1/2 *teaspoon caster sugar*
salt, pepper
4oz/115g *black olives, pitted*
1 *heaped dessertspoon marjoram*
  leaves

Prepare this tart in an oblong tray such as a Swiss roll tin (you may have extra dough). Press the tines of a fork around the edge of the dough to make a pattern.

Peel the onions, halve and thinly slice them. Heat a tablespoon of olive oil in a frying pan and sweat the onions with the thyme over a low heat for 30 minutes. Reserve them in a bowl.

Peel and thinly slice the garlic. Add the remaining oil to the frying pan and cook the garlic for a minute until it releases its aroma. Add the tomatoes, the purée, sugar and seasoning and cook until it reduces to a fairly dry purée. Depending on the sweetness of the tomatoes it may require a little extra sugar.

Preheat the oven to 200°C/400°F/Gas 6. Spread the onions on the base of the pizza, spread the tomato purée on top and bake for 25 minutes. Halve the olives and scatter these over the cooked pizza, brush with olive oil, then scatter the marjoram leaves over. It can be eaten hot or cold.

Aubergine and Goat's Cheese Pizza with Roasted Garlic

This pizza is big and bright, with bold splashes of colour. Prepare the peppers and the garlic ahead of time, at the same time as making the dough. Usually I make this recipe up as two large 11 inch/27cm pizzas.

---

6 small red and orange peppers
6 garlic cloves
extra virgin olive oil
a few basil leaves
salt, pepper
2 aubergines
8oz/225g medium-matured goat's
  cheese

1 quantity of pizza dough
(see page 109)
2 tablespoons traditional pesto
(see page 222, about a quarter
of recipe)

The peppers and garlic can be cooked at the same time. Preheat the oven to its highest setting and roast the peppers for 20 minutes. Place one plastic bag inside another, place the peppers inside, seal the bag and allow them to steam as they cool. Peel and thickly slice the garlic cloves, blanch them for 1 minute in boiling water, then place them in a foil package with 1 tablespoon of olive oil. Twist the foil edges into a parcel and place this in the oven for 20 minutes also.

Peel and deseed the peppers. Layer them in a container with a little olive oil and the basil, roughly torn, seasoning each layer. Leave this to steep in the fridge for several hours, or while the dough is proving.

To prepare the aubergines heat the griddle, slice them ¹/₂ inch/1cm thick, brush the slices with olive oil on one side, grill this side until streaked with charring, brush the upper side with oil, season and grill, and reserve the slices. Slice the goat's cheese.

Preheat the oven to 200°C/400°F/Gas 6. Arrange the ingredients on the bread bases to within ¹/₂ inch/1cm of the rim. Lay the peppers and aubergines down first, then the goat's cheese slices on top. Scatter the garlic over. Cook the pizza for 20 minutes, when the edges should be golden and crusty. Thin the pesto with olive oil until it is a thick pouring consistency and trickle it over the cooked pizza.

Eat the pizza while it is hot, or warm.

Calzone with Leeks, Thyme and Provolone

A calzone is basically a stuffed pizza, looking much the same as a Cornish pasty. They are not especially elegant fare, and are nicest eaten warm from the oven. The dough will absorb any moisture in the filling as they cool, making them go soggy. I also prefer the casing to be rolled very thinly.

---

3 garlic cloves
1lb 10oz/750g leeks, trimmed
  weight
1 tablespoon extra virgin olive oil
1¹/₂oz/45g unsalted butter
1 heaped teaspoon thyme
salt, pepper
6oz/170g butternut squash,
  weight excluding skin

6oz/170g demi-sec goat's cheese
3oz/85g Provolone
1 quantity of pizza dough
  (see page 109)
1 egg (size 2), beaten
extra virgin olive oil

Mince the garlic cloves. Halve the leeks lengthwise and slice. Heat the olive oil and 1oz of the butter in a large frying pan and add the garlic. When it gives off an aroma add the leeks, the thyme and seasoning. Cook for approximately 8 minutes stirring frequently, until they are soft and cooked, but not coloured. Remove to a bowl and cool. Thinly slice the squash. Melt the remaining butter in the frying pan and sweat the squash for 3-4 minutes until just soft. Add to the leeks and allow to cool. Break the goat's cheese into ¹/₂in/1cm cubes and grate the Provolone. Mix the cheeses with the leeks and adjust the seasoning.

Divide the pizza dough into 6, roll each piece to a circle 9 inches/22cm in diameter, and leave to rest for 20 minutes.

Preheat the oven to 200°C/400°F/Gas 6. Place some of the filling on one half of each circle. Beat the egg with 1 dessertspoon of water and paint the perimeter of each dough circle which surrounds the filling. Fold the unfilled half on top of the filled half. Press the edges together and trim with a pastry cutter. Lightly brush the surface of the calzone with the olive oil and bake for 12-15 minutes until pale gold, but not too crisp.

Calzone with Broccoli and Gorgonzola

Prepare these calzone according to the recipe above, using the following filling.

---

2 garlic cloves	*salt, pepper*
14oz/400g broccoli, trimmed	*6oz/170g aubergine*
weight	*3oz/85g sun-dried tomatoes*
6 tablespoons extra virgin olive oil	*8oz/225g Gorgonzola*
½ teaspoon chilli, finely	
chopped	

Mince the garlic and cut the broccoli into ½ inch/1cm florets. Heat 4 tablespoons of olive oil in a large frying pan, add the garlic and chilli, and moments later add the broccoli and season it. Cook for 3 minutes, stirring frequently, then add 1 tablespoon water, turn the heat right down, cover the pan and steam the broccoli for about 3 minutes – it should be cooked but firm. Remove it to a bowl. Cube the aubergine. Heat the remaining oil in the frying pan and cook the aubergine for 6 minutes until soft and coloured. Add to the broccoli and leave to cool. Cut the sun-dried tomatoes into strips and dice the Gorgonzola; add these to the vegetables and adjust seasoning.

Empanadas

The Galician empanada would seem to be closely related to the Italian '*sfinciuni*', found in Palermo, though the character and filling of each differs according to the region. Basically it is a pie enclosed by two spheres of dough. Smaller empanadillas, similar to a calzone, can also be made. Xavier Domingo accords considerable significance to the empanada in *A Taste of Spain*: 'An empanada is essentially a pastry with a filling, and in Galicia that filling can consist of almost anything: eel, lamprey, salt cod with raisins, cockles, scallops, sardines or xouba, conger eel, mussels, onion, garlic, tomato, chilli peppers, veal, pork, thrush, quail or rabbit . . . This delicious pastry or bread stuffed with a filling that bakes along with the dough is so much a part of Galicia's cuisine that it is impossible to imagine a Galician meal without empanadas being served at some point along the way. Empanadas, to my way of thinking, represent the initial qualitative leap from the minimal cooking of bread, oil and garlic into the realm of more sophisticated, complex cuisine. Empanadas are the first step across the threshold between pure breadmaking and the rest of the culinary universe.'

Empanada with Caramelized Onions, Cabbage and Chestnuts, with a Butter Sauce

The dough for this empanada lies somewhere between a pastry and a bread. Less chewy than a bread, it has a pleasant crumbly side to it. It is a deep pie, to be served in slices; it does require its butter sauce, and does need to be served hot.

Dried chestnuts have a smoky flavour, and the soaking liquor is useful for sauces, so in this instance they are preferable to fresh ones and certainly easier to prepare. They can usually be found in health-food shops.

Filling

4oz/115g dried chestnuts	salt, pepper
2¹/₂lb/1.1kg Spanish onions	1 Savoy cabbage
1oz/30g unsalted butter	white vegetable fat for greasing

Empanada dough

1lb 2oz/500g plain flour	1 egg (size 2), beaten
1 level teaspoon salt	3fl oz/55ml extra virgin olive oil
¹/₂ teaspoon caster sugar	3fl oz/55ml milk
1 teaspoon dried yeast	3fl oz/55ml warm water

To glaze

1 egg (size 2), beaten with 1 tablespoon water

Butter sauce

5fl oz/150ml red wine	*reduced liquor from*
9oz/250g unsalted butter	*soaking chestnuts*
salt, pepper	

Soak the chestnuts in plentiful water overnight.

Place the flour, salt, sugar and yeast in the bowl of a food processor, add the egg, then with the motor running add the olive oil, the milk and gradually add the water – it may not take the full amount to bind the dough. Knead the dough for several minutes until it is smooth and elastic. You can do this in the food processor, but if you do it by hand knead for around 8 minutes. Place the dough in an oiled bowl, slash the surface with a cross to facilitate its rising, and cover loosely with a plastic bag. Leave to rise in a warm place for 2 hours.

Drain the chestnuts and boil for 45 minutes. Remove them to a bowl and quarter them once they are cool. Reduce the cooking liquor to a few tablespoons and reserve.

Peel, halve and thinly slice the onions. Use two pans to cook them – if they are overcrowded they will stew. Heat half the butter in each pan and cook the onions over a very low heat for 1 hour until they are soft and creamy, though not coloured. They will require quite dutiful attention to ensure they do not catch and burn. Combine the onions in one pan, turn the heat up and cook, stirring almost constantly, until they are golden and caramelized. Season them.

Discard the outer leaves of the cabbage and separate the remaining leaves, reserving the heart for some other use. Cut the hard white centre from each leaf. Bring a large pan of salted water to the boil and cook the leaves for 3 minutes, then plunge them into cold water, drain on kitchen paper and reserve.

Preheat the oven to 200°C/400°F/Gas 6. Grease a 10 inch/25cm spring-form cake tin with the vegetable fat. Punch the dough down and knead it until smooth. Flour a worksurface, divide the dough, and roll one half to fit the tin and come up the sides; line the tin with this. Spread half the onions on the base, then half the chestnuts. Lay a double layer of cabbage leaves over, season, and arrange the remaining onions and chestnuts on top. Roll the other half of the dough to fit the top. Pinch the edges together, trim the excess leaving a ½ inch/1cm rim, then press this level with the top of the pie using a fork. Paint the surface with the beaten egg mixture and bake for 25 minutes.

While the pie is baking, make the sauce: reduce the red wine to a couple of tablespoons, then gradually whisk in the butter, in cubes. Season and add the reduced chestnut cooking liquor. Remove the collar from the pie and serve hot in large wedges with some of the sauce spooned around it.

Bruschetta with Parsley Pesto and Aubergine Salad

I wonder how an Englishman might feel if on visiting Rome, every menu of every restaurant had a version of a cucumber sandwich charged at a price no self-respecting Brit would care to pay. It must seem strange for the visiting Italian to find on the menu of each restaurant visited, with a modish Italian bent, an ever more glorious version of the bruschetta. I have only once eaten a genuine bruschetta and it remains the most memorable: a small café in a Tuscan village, a tray of bruschetta clearly designed to utilize yesterday's bread and a glut of over-ripe tomatoes. A thick slice of coarse-textured white bread, toasted, rubbed with garlic, olive oil trickled over and the chopped tomatoes seeping into the toast, the whole thing a delicious semi-soggy treat.

This parsley pesto is a variation on the classic Italian version, and is made with equal quantities of basil and flat-leaf parsley, omitting the Parmesan. The result is a thick, pale green paste – not as pungent as the original, it can be consumed in greater quantity. Use it cold as a sauce or mixed with home-made mayonnaise. It is good thickly spread on a bruschetta, mounded with some grilled Italianate vegetables: aubergine, courgettes, fennel, mushrooms, red onions or peppers. It has a special affinity with aubergines and tomatoes, as this recipe illustrates.

Parsley pesto

The herbs should be washed, and you should select a mild-tasting olive oil – if you are using a stronger one, then use some arachide oil or another tasteless oil in with it. Liquidizing this pesto takes a bit of doing and the resulting paste is very thick, so do not give up half-way through by adding some liquid

1 shallot	4fl oz/115ml extra virgin
2oz/55g pine nuts	olive oil
2oz/55g flat-leaf parsley, stripped	salt, pepper
from stalk	lemon juice
2oz/55g basil leaves	

Coarsely chop the shallot and place it together with the pine nuts, half the herbs, the olive oil and seasoning in a liquidizer. Reduce this to a purée, cautiously pushing the leaves towards the blade while it is running, using a long-handled spoon. Incorporate the remaining leaves when appropriate. Adjust the seasoning and add lemon juice to taste. The pesto firms to a spreadable consistency on chilling.

Bruschetta

1 aubergine	6 thick slices coarse-textured
salt	white bread
3 marmande tomatoes	1 garlic clove
extra virgin olive oil	extra virgin olive oil
pepper	flat-leaf parsley to garnish
lemon juice	

Cut the aubergine into ¼ inch/0.5cm cubes. Sprinkle them with salt and leave in a colander for 30 minutes to exude their juices. Skin and deseed the tomatoes (see page 10). Cut them into ¼ inch/0.5cm dice and place in a bowl.

Rinse and pat dry the aubergine. Heat a little olive oil in a frying pan and cook the cubes to a smoky brown. Remove them to a bowl, and once they are cool mix them with the tomatoes. Dress the salad with olive oil, seasoning it with salt, pepper and lemon juice. It is best made as close to the time of serving as possible. If this is not appropriate, then some halved cherry tomatoes and grilled slices of aubergine would be a better option.

Toast the bread on a griddle. Give one side a cursory rub with the garlic clove and dribble some olive oil over. Spread each slice generously with the pesto, top with a mound of the aubergine and tomato salad and garnish with a few leaves of flat-leaf parsley. Eat straight away.

Molletes filled with Goat's Cheese and Roasted Pepper

Molletes are small oval-shaped Spanish rolls. In Seville there is a tiny street-corner bar, La Tienda, which sells excellent cheeses, hams, wines, oils and superior sherry vinegars. Along the bar sit bottles of various fortified wines, in curious hues of pink, red and green. A house speciality are *molletes*: little toasted rolls filled with a variety of ingredients such as goat's cheese, spicy peppers, anchovies and cured meats. I came across toasted *molletes* in other bars, but nowhere as good as at La Tienda.

To prepare a *mollete*, preheat the grill, take a small soft white roll, halve it and dribble some olive oil over the cut surfaces. Place slices of goat's cheese in the centre and a few strips of grilled red pepper. Close the roll and toast it under the grill for a couple of minutes, turning it as the top starts to brown so as to toast the base. The *mollete* should be hot and crisp on the outside, the cheese inside warm, but not melted.

Quail's Eggs in Herb Mayonnaise on Toast

If peeling quail's eggs feels like penance, then substitute 6 hen's eggs.

Mayonnaise

1oz/30g watercress	*1 egg yolk (size 2)*
1 heaped tablespoon coriander	*5fl oz/150ml arachide oil*
leaves	*1 spring onion, finely chopped*
1 heaped tablespoon dill fronds	*salt*
1 heaped tablespoon chervil fronds	*lemon juice*

---

24 quail's eggs	*finely chopped chives to garnish*
4 thick slices white bread	

To prepare the mayonnaise, first wash and then chop together the watercress, coriander, dill and chervil. Place these in a cloth and squeeze out any water. Whisk the egg yolk and continue whisking while adding the arachide oil in a slow stream. The resulting mayonnaise should be very thick. Add the chopped herbs and watercress, and the spring onion. Season the mayonnaise with salt and lemon juice.

Boil the quail's eggs for $3\frac{1}{2}$ minutes. Cool them in a bowl of cold water. Shell them and reserve in cold water until required. Quarter the eggs, reserve a few quarters as a garnish, and mix the rest into the mayonnaise.

To serve, toast the bread and pile some egg mayonnaise on to each slice. Place the reserved egg quarters in the centre and scatter over some chopped chives.

Mushrooms, Pecan Nuts and Beetroot on Sourdough Bread

Use any German rye bread or sourdough bread for this recipe. Obtain the onion juice by compressing a chunk of onion in a garlic press.

1oz/30g pecan nuts	*3oz/85g button mushrooms*
4oz/115g cream cheese	*4 slices sourdough bread*
lemon juice	*black pepper*
1/2 teaspoon onion juice	*walnut oil*
salt, cayenne pepper	*chopped chives and dill*
1 beetroot, cooked	

Mince the pecan nuts. Work these into the cream cheese, together with lemon juice to taste, the onion juice, salt and cayenne pepper.

Slice the beetroot into julienne strips about 1 1/2 inches/4cm long. Wipe and slice the mushrooms.

Toast the bread and spread some of the cream cheese mixture on each slice. Arrange some sliced mushrooms on top of this, season with salt and pepper and place some beetroot on top of the mushrooms. Drizzle over a little walnut oil and sprinkle with chopped herbs.

Pitta Breads filled with Feta, Herbs and Sun-dried Tomatoes

No salt or pepper is required here: the olive oil adds a note of pepper and the cheese and sun-dried tomatoes lend their saltiness.

---

4 spring onions
4 halves sun-dried tomatoes
2 tablespoons flat-leaf parsley
  leaves
2 tablespoons coriander leaves

extra virgin olive oil
5oz/140g feta cheese
4 tomatoes
4 pitta breads

Trim and slice the spring onions and cut the sun-dried tomatoes into strips. Mix together the onions, sun-dried tomatoes and herbs in a bowl with 4 tablespoons of olive oil. Slice the feta and cut it into blocks about 1½ x 1 inch/4 x 2cm. Add these to the bowl.

Skin the tomatoes by plunging them into boiling water for 30 seconds and then into cold water. Slice them thinly, discarding the end slices containing the core.

Heat the pitta breads on both sides under the grill. They may puff up, and should emit a cloud of steam as you slit them open. They should be slightly crisp but retain their toothsome quality. Dribble some olive oil over the cut surface of each lower half, arrange some sliced tomatoes over and then the herb and feta mixture, and enclose with the top half of pitta. Halve and serve.

Scorzonera Croustades with Fines Herbes

Long, black and rather brutish in appearance, scorzonera and the paler skinned salsify have never become commonplace in this country. Perhaps it is the preparation which puts people off, though it is not especially irksome. Scorzonera is a winter vegetable and the flavour is most reminiscent of Jerusalem artichokes; in fact, these would make a very pleasant substitute. Scorzonera is also known as black salsify, black oyster plant and viper grass – the plant juices were once used to provide relief from snakebite.

Scorzonera has to be peeled; this is most easily done under running water, wearing rubber gloves to avoid staining your hands. Then cook it immediately in a pan of water containing lemon juice and a little flour to keep it white, otherwise it should be stored in acidulated water. Beware when you are cooking it, since like a Jerusalem artichoke it progresses from being perfectly cooked to mushy in a fleeting moment.

Strictly speaking the sauce in this recipe is a 'velouté', similar to a basic white sauce or béchamel, but part of the liquid used is stock (in this case vegetable stock). This eases the 'gloopy' nature these sauces can take on, and enlivens the flavour which can otherwise lack dimension. I would use this particular recipe wherever I needed a cheese or white sauce, and use whatever flavourings or additions were appropriate.

Sauce

2oz/55g *unsalted butter*	5oz/140g *Gruyère, grated*
1¹/₂oz/45g *plain flour*	*salt, pepper*
6fl oz/175ml *milk*	1 *heaped tablespoon fines herbes*
6fl oz/175ml *double cream*	*(parsley, chives, chervil,*
4fl oz/115ml *reduced vegetable*	*tarragon)*
stock (see page 10)	

Croustades

---

6 *thin slices rye bread*	2lb/900g *scorzonera*
2oz/55g *unsalted butter, melted*	1oz/30g *sorrel*
juice of ¹/₂ *lemon*	¹/₂oz/15g *unsalted butter*
1 *teaspoon plain flour*	

First prepare the sauce. Melt the butter in a saucepan, add the flour and cook the roux for a couple of minutes. Gradually incorporate the milk, cream and stock and cook the sauce for 5 minutes, stirring. Add the grated cheese and season with salt and pepper. Stir in the herbs just before the sauce is used.

Preheat the oven to 200°C/400°F/Gas 6. Prepare the croustades by lightly brushing each slice of bread with the butter, on both sides. Lay these on a baking tray and cook them for 10-15 minutes until they are golden and crisp. These can be cooked in advance and reheated for a couple of minutes when required.

Bring a large pan of water to the boil with the lemon juice and flour. Wearing rubber gloves to avoid staining your hands, peel the scorzonera, cut it into strips the length of the croustades and halve them lengthwise if thick. Place in a bowl of acidulated water if not cooking immediately. Boil for 12-15 minutes. Drain the scorzonera and dress with the sauce.

If the sorrel leaves are large, cut them into broad strips. Melt the butter for the sorrel in a small frying pan, add the sorrel and cook momentarily until it wilts. Arrange some of the scorzonera on the warm rye toast, and place a few leaves of the sorrel on each one.

See also:

French Onion Soup 'Gratinée' (page 32)

Chopped Olives on Bruschetta with a Salad of Rocket, Watercress and Parmesan (page 45)

Eggs Florentine (page 59)

Welsh Rarebit (page 76)

Baked Goat's Cheese with Roasted Garlic, and Focaccia with Coriander and Rocket (page 81)

Gratin of Celery with Lovage and Truffle Oil, served with Parmesan and Chilli Muffins (page 87)

Ploughman's with a Sweet Tomato and Sesame Chutney (page 90)

Char-grilled Tofu with Aromatics, and Tapenade Toast (page 144)

Char-grilled Aubergine and Salsa on Fried Bread (page 185)

Pulses, Beans and Grains

Bissara

This broad bean purée is traditional to the hills of Morocco and Algeria. The type of paprika used is important: use a sweet paprika with a smoky flavour, as other varieties might prove too hot in the quantity specified here. While fresh broad beans are preferable, frozen beans are perfectly adequate. This purée goes well with the mezze dishes on page 54. Serve it with warm pitta bread.

1¹/₂ lb/675g broad beans
³/₄ teaspoon green chilli, chopped
1 level teaspoon cumin seeds,
 freshly ground
1 teaspoon paprika

1 garlic clove, chopped
7 tablespoons olive oil
juice of 1 small lemon
salt, pepper

To serve

olive oil
lemon juice
paprika

If using frozen broad beans, boil them for 3-4 minutes. If using fresh broad beans, boil them for 8 minutes.

In the bowl of a food processor place the beans, the chilli, the cumin, the paprika and the chopped garlic. Reduce to a purée, trickling in the olive oil and lemon juice. Season the purée with salt and pepper and pass through a sieve. Place it in a shallow dish. Serve it at room temperature: trickle some olive oil over the surface, some lemon juice, and a sprinkling of paprika.

Hummus

While at university, my brother fuelled many a dinner party with a bowl of hummus and he kindly sent me a copy of his recipe and variations thereof, from which I have developed this version. I have scaled it down to feed a conservative 4-6 people. Serve this with other mezze (page 54), or simply as an appetizer with pitta bread warmed in the oven.

8oz/225g chickpeas
2 dessertspoons light tahina paste
1 garlic clove, coarsely chopped
1 level teaspoon cumin, freshly
  ground

2fl oz/55ml lemon juice
6 tablespoons extra virgin olive oil
salt, pepper

To serve

extra virgin olive oil
cayenne pepper
toasted sesame seeds

Soak the chickpeas in plenty of water overnight. Boil them for 1½ hours, drain, cover and leave them to cool.

In the bowl of a food processor place the chickpeas, tahina paste, coarsely chopped garlic clove, and cumin. With the motor running add the lemon juice, the olive oil and sufficient water to render the mixture a smooth, thick cream. Season the hummus and place it in a shallow dish. Trickle a little olive oil on the surface, add a dusting of cayenne pepper and scatter over toasted sesame seeds.

Falafel

Falafel can be heavy, so I have added quinoa to lighten them. The falafel do require some sort of a sauce, and they are perfect as part of a selection of mezze (see page 54) which includes creamy purées. I have used Claudia Roden's recipe in *A New Book of Middle Eastern Food* as the basis for this version. The dried white broad beans can be found in good continental delicatessens.

6oz/170g *dried white broad beans, skinned*	2 *heaped tablespoons coriander, finely chopped*
3oz/85g *quinoa*	$^1/_2$ *teaspoon baking powder*
1 *shallot*	$^1/_2$ *teaspoon dried yeast*
1 *garlic clove*	*cayenne pepper*
salt	2 *eggs (size 2), beaten*
$^3/_4$ *teaspoon cumin seeds*	*fine dry breadcrumbs*
$^3/_4$ *teaspoon coriander seeds*	*arachide oil for deep-frying*

Soak the dried broad beans in plenty of water overnight. Drain and rinse them and reduce to a purée in a food processor. This takes some working at: the mixture needs to be sticky for it to hold together well. Remove to a large bowl.

Boil the quinoa in salted water for 15 minutes. Drain it and combine it with the bean purée. Finely dice the shallot, and chop and crush the garlic to a paste with some salt. Grind the spices in a pestle and mortar and combine all the ingredients except the last three, seasoning with salt and cayenne pepper. Form into balls the size of a walnut between the palms of your hands, place on a tray or plate, cover loosely with clingfilm and let stand for 1 hour. Dip each falafel into beaten egg and roll in breadcrumbs.

Heat the oil to 160°C/325°F (you can test the temperature using a jam thermometer). Deep-fry the falafel for 4-5 minutes until lightly golden. Drain on kitchen paper and serve straight away.

Pasta and Bean Soup with Extra Virgin Olive Oil and Parmesan

I live in hope of one day being able to buy in this country some of the exotic fresh pulses you find in northern Italian markets, like the purple pods containing fresh borlotti beans, exquisitely marbled in cream and purple. In taste they are sweet and chestnut-like, delicious simply boiled, with some olive oil poured over, seasoned and coarsely mashed on the plate with a fork. Pasta and beans are perfect partners: the silky texture of one and the dry and sweet nature of the other. By itself the soup is bland, so the quality of the oil and the Parmesan are all-important.

---

2 tablespoons extra virgin olive oil
1 onion, chopped
2 garlic cloves, halved
7oz/200g dried borlotti or pinto beans, soaked overnight
2 tablespoons flat-leaf parsley, finely chopped
1 stick celery, sliced

1 marmande tomato, peeled, seeded and diced
1 sprig rosemary
3 pints/1.7 litres light vegetable stock or water
salt, pepper
5oz/140g macaroni or other tubular pasta

To serve

extra virgin olive oil
freshly grated Parmesan

Heat the oil in a large saucepan and cook the onion and garlic for 3 minutes. Add the beans, half the parsley, the celery, tomato, rosemary and stock or water, and simmer, covered, for 1½ hours. Discard the rosemary, reserve a third of the beans, liquidize the remaining soup and return to the saucepan with the reserved beans. Season, add the pasta, and simmer until cooked. Stir in the remaining parsley and allow to stand for 5 minutes. Serve with plenty of olive oil and Parmesan.

Orzotto ai Porcini

The food of Trentino in Northern Italy is substantial, influenced by the Venetians, Lombardy and the Austrians. '*Zuppe d'orzo*' is a soup made with pearl barley, thick and heartening with the addition of various vegetables. An *orzotto* is an inspired dish of recent origin in the area. Quite simply it is a risotto made with pearl barley; the method differs from a rice-based risotto and it demands less attention. Barley and porcini go together beautifully; I have eaten it accompanied by '*schiacciata al semi di finocchio*', a circular, flat bread sold locally, not unlike a ciabatta in texture, but studded with fennel seeds and leavened with beer.

10^{1}/$_{2}$oz/300g pearl barley
1oz/30g dried porcini
mushroom soaking liquor made up
   to 1 pint/600ml with vegetable
   stock
2 tablespoons extra virgin olive oil

2 garlic cloves, minced
3fl oz/85ml white wine
^{1}/$_{2}$oz/15g unsalted butter
2fl oz/55ml double cream
2oz/55g freshly grated Parmesan
salt, pepper

Soak the barley overnight in plenty of water. Boil for 15 minutes, then drain it. Soak the porcini in $^{1}/_{2}$ pint/300ml of boiling water for 15 minutes. Bring the mushroom liquor and stock to the boil. Heat the olive oil in a saucepan, cook the garlic momentarily until it gives off an aroma, add the barley, porcini and wine, and cook for a couple of minutes. Add all the boiling liquor and simmer for 15 minutes, stirring occasionally, until it is the consistency of a risotto. Stir in the butter, cream and Parmesan, and season well.

Spinach with Chickpeas and Spices

'*Espinacas con garbanzos*' is a popular tapa in Andalusia. It is deliciously rich and spiced, and typically Moorish with its overtones of cumin, coriander and saffron. I ate a memorable dish of it in a small tapas bar just off San Lorenzo in Seville, called El Retablo, which has an adjoining dining-room. A small windowless room with a handful of tables covered in plastic, it has a good reputation for its food and caters specifically for the Sevillian. The only other people in the dining-room on our visit were a merry foursome of gents, enjoying Saturday lunch without the constriction of wives or children: brandy was ordered by the bottle.

1¹/₄ lb/550g fresh young spinach
  leaves
extra virgin olive oil
2 garlic cloves, finely chopped
2 shallots, finely chopped
¹/₂ teaspoon cumin seeds, freshly
  ground
¹/₂ teaspoon coriander seeds, freshly
  ground

5 saffron filaments, roasted and
  ground (see page 9)
5oz/140g cooked chickpeas
10oz/285g tomatoes, peeled, seeded
  and diced
salt, pepper
lemon juice

Wash and dry the spinach thoroughly, removing any browned stalks. Heat a tablespoon of olive oil in a saucepan, throw in a large handful of spinach and cook it until it wilts. Remove it to a bowl and cook the remaining spinach in the same fashion. Drain the spinach and discard any water that has collected before using it in the next stage.

Heat a little more olive oil in a medium saucepan and cook the garlic and shallots until they are soft. Add the ground spices and chickpeas and cook them for a minute. Return the spinach to the pan with the tomato concassée and seasoning. Cover the pan and braise it over a low heat for 10 minutes. Add an additional tablespoon of olive oil and cook uncovered for a further 10 minutes so that any remaining liquid evaporates.

Adjust the seasoning and sharpen the dish with a squeeze of lemon juice. In Spain this would be served with little crackers.

Char-grilled Tofu with Aromatics, and Tapenade Toast

The very mention of tofu activates a chorus of alarm bells in my culinary imagination. Determined to overcome this prejudice, my conclusion after experimenting with it is that it must be woven into a dish positively gyrating with character and flavour, and must be cooked to achieve a crisp exterior. However, I shall continue to pick it out of salads in its raw and untampered-with state.

---

15 saffron filaments	1 teaspoon thyme
1 red pepper	2 teaspoons basil, chopped
1/2 yellow pepper	2fl oz/55ml extra virgin olive oil
1 small onion	2fl oz/55ml white wine
2 inner sticks of celery	6fl oz/175ml water
1 small courgette	salt, pepper
1 small fennel bulb	1 1/4lb/550g tofu
1 large garlic clove	extra virgin olive oil

Toast the saffron in a dry frying pan for 1 minute, then grind it in a pestle and mortar and infuse with a little boiling water.

Peel the peppers using a potato peeler, then deseed them and dice the flesh minutely. Dice the remaining vegetables, including the garlic, in the same fashion, and place them together with the peppers, thyme, chopped basil, olive oil, wine, water and seasoning into a pan. Cover, and simmer for 15 minutes on a low heat, adding the saffron tincture 5 minutes before the end.

Slice the tofu, place it in a container and spoon the aromatics over. Leave this to marinate for several hours or overnight. Remove the tofu slices and scrape off any vegetables from the marinade. Heat the griddle, brush the tofu with olive oil and season it; grill it on both sides until the exterior is crisp in places and brown. Heat the aromatics in a small pan and serve the tofu slices on a bed of the aromatics accompanied by the croûtons and tapenade cream.

Tapenade Toast

4oz/115g black olives, pitted	*¹/₂ garlic clove*
¹/₂ oz/15g capers	*1 tablespoon extra virgin olive oil*
pinch thyme	*black pepper*
1 teaspoon brandy (optional)	*1 tablespoon crème fraîche*

Croûtons

1 small stick French bread	*olive oil*

Purée all the ingredients for the tapenade together in a food processor, until they are a thick paste.

Slice the bread thinly and lay the croûtons on a baking sheet. Place in the oven at 180°C/350°F/Gas 4 for 5 minutes until they have dried out. Paint each side sparingly with olive oil and return to the oven for a further 10-12 minutes or until they are golden-brown. Cool on paper parchment before storing.

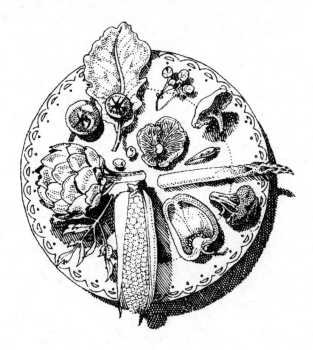

Tarts and Pies

Potato and Onion Tart with Horseradish Cream

The base of this tart is spread with a sweet onion purée, followed by a layer of sliced potatoes, then crème fraîche flavoured with fresh horseradish is smoothed over. It is perfect eaten on its own; a salad or suitable vegetable dish could be served afterwards.

Fresh horseradish is essential. Until recently this remained a gardener's treat, which is absurd given its tenacity and ability to grow. Of late a number of supermarkets have started to sell it.

3lb/1.4kg Spanish onions
1¹/₂oz/45g unsalted butter
salt, pepper
2¹/₄lb/1kg new potatoes
1 tablespoon extra virgin olive oil

9oz/250g puff pastry
2 heaped teaspoons fresh
* horseradish, finely grated*
7fl oz/200ml crème fraîche
1 egg (size 2) for glazing

Peel, halve and slice the onions. Melt 1oz/30g of butter in a heavy-bottomed saucepan, add the onions, cover the pan and cook them over a very low heat for 1 hour. Stir regularly to check they are not sticking to the base of the pan. Remove the lid, season them, and cook off any excess juices.

Select potatoes of roughly the same size, peel them, bring a large pan of salted water to the boil and cook for 10 minutes. Drain and let the surface water evaporate. Heat the olive oil and the remaining ¹/₂oz/15g of butter in a frying pan and cook the potatoes in a single layer until golden on all sides. Leave them to cool to room temperature.

Roll the puff pastry $^1/_8$ inch/0.25cm thick and line a 10 inch/25cm tart tin $1^1/_2$ inches/4cm deep; run a rolling pin over the rim to remove the excess pastry. Prick the base with a fork and line the case with foil and baking beans. Cook it for 25-30 minutes at 180°C/350°F/Gas 4, until it is lightly golden. Remove the foil and beans.

Slice the potatoes as thinly as possible, discarding the end slices – a serrated knife gives good results. Spread the onions on the base of the case. Arrange potato slices in concentric circles, working outwards. Season this layer. Stir the grated horseradish into the crème fraîche, season it and spoon over the potatoes. Whisk the egg with 1 tablespoon of water and brush the pastry rim. Bake the tart for 30-35 minutes at 180°C/350°F/Gas 4. The surface should be golden in places – give it a minute or two under the grill if necessary.

Carrots with Rosemary and Lancashire Cheese in a Suet Crust

I shall not set about trying to convert anyone to the suet crust. While distorted versions of it remain uppermost in the minds of many people sustained by memories of the school dinner, it is something that either does or does not appeal. Personally I love suet puddings, and they are extremely good-natured and simple to make.

There is no call for a sauce or accompaniment with this dish – it is well-balanced as it stands. It would be more appropriate to have another small course either before or after it.

Suet crust

12oz/340g self-raising flour 6oz/170g shredded vegetable suet	salt, pepper

1lb 6oz/625g baby carrots,
  2-3 inches/5-7cm long and
  1/4 inch/0.5cm thick
1oz/30g unsalted butter
4 sprigs rosemary
salt, pepper
	1lb/450g fresh spinach
	3/4oz/20g unsalted butter
	2 eggs (size 2)
	4fl oz/115ml double cream
	4oz/115g Lancashire cheese

To make the suet crust, place the flour, suet and seasoning together in a bowl, bring the dough together with water and knead it until smooth. Wrap it in clingfilm and rest in the fridge for 30 minutes.

Top and tail the baby carrots. Heat the butter in a large saucepan or frying pan with a lid. Add the carrots and cook for 5 minutes. Add the rosemary, season and add 6 tablespoons of water. Cover the pan with its lid, turn the heat down low and stew the carrots for 5 minutes. If any liquid remains, turn the heat up and cook without lid until it evaporates. Discard the rosemary.

Wash the spinach, removing any tough stalks. Heat a knob of butter in a saucepan, throw in some spinach and toss until it wilts. Cover the pan and cook the spinach for a minute longer. Reserve the cooked spinach in a bowl and season it. Cook the remaining leaves in the same fashion. Drain off any excess liquid before using it in the next stage.

Whisk the eggs and pass them through a sieve, then stir in the cream. Grate the cheese and add this also. Combine the carrots and spinach and mix with the cream mixture.

Lightly oil a 3 pint/1.7 litre pudding basin. Roll the suet pastry 1/4 inch/0.5cm thick, reserving some dough for the lid, and line the basin. Spoon in the vegetable mixture. Roll the remaining pastry into a lid and cover the pie. Pinch the edges together and trim the excess. Cover the basin tightly with foil and secure with string. Choose a saucepan large enough to hold the basin, and fill with water so it will come two-thirds of the way up the sides of the basin. Bring the water to the boil, place the basin inside, cover with the lid and steam over a low heat for 2 hours.

To serve the pudding, run a knife around the edge of the basin and turn the pudding out. Serve it in slices, either hot or warm.

Goat's Cheese Tart 'Fines Herbes'

I suppose that this is fundamentally a quiche, but there is no need for a quiche to mean thick pastry and solid custard: the custard in this recipe is rich and very light and creamy, which has to do with the proportion of eggs used. It is a shallow tart, and well flavoured. The shortcrust pastry recipe is taken from *Cooking for Friends* by Raymond Blanc.

Pastry

1 egg yolk (size 2)	2¹/₂ fl oz/75ml water
¹/₂ teaspoon caster sugar	9oz/250g plain flour, sifted
¹/₂ teaspoon salt	2¹/₂ oz/70g unsalted butter, diced

Filling

4 eggs (size 5)	6oz/170g mature goat's cheese,
1 egg yolk (size 5)	rind removed
7fl oz/200ml milk	10oz/285g marmande tomatoes
7fl oz/200ml double cream	(approx 1¹/₂), skinned, seeded
salt, pepper	and diced
2 heaped tablespoons fines herbes,	3 spring onions
finely chopped	

To prepare the pastry mix together the egg yolk, sugar, salt and water. Combine the flour and butter in a food processor until the mixture resembles fine crumbs. Bring the dough together with the egg and water solution and knead it for a few minutes with a sprinkling of flour, then wrap it in clingfilm and rest it in the fridge for 45 minutes.

Butter and flour a 10 inch/25cm tart case 1¹/₂ inches/4cm deep with a removable base. Lightly flour a worksurface, knead the pastry until it softens, then roll it ¹/₈ inch/0.25cm thick and line the case. Trim it allowing ¹/₈ inch/0.25cm above the top of the rim for shrinkage. Chill the case for 30 minutes. Heat the oven to 200°C/400°F/Gas 6, line the case with foil and baking beans and cook for 15 minutes. Remove the foil and beans and cook for another 10 minutes until just starting to colour.

Whisk together the eggs, egg yolk, milk and cream. Season the custard and stir in the chopped herbs. Dice the goat's cheese into ¹/₂ inch/1cm cubes. Scatter these over the base of the case. Distribute the tomato concassée on top. Trim the spring onions, thinly slice, and scatter these over. Pour over the custard and bake the tart for 30-35 minutes in the preheated oven, until the custard is set and the surface is starting to colour. Remove the collar of the tart case and serve in large wedges.

Courgette Tart

I ate a version of this courgette tart at the Walnut Tree Inn in Abergavenny, Wales. It is easy to see why this restaurant has been such a success for so long. The interior is refreshingly unpretentious, like the food, which is always imaginative and beautifully cooked. The welcoming presence of the Taruschios makes any visitor feel as though they have come home. This tart was served with a tomato sauce and a fritter of a courgette flower, stuffed with mozzarella, a little Parmesan and herbs. There is a similar recipe for courgette flowers stuffed with mozzarella, tomato and basil on page 179. I like this tart when it has cooled for 15 minutes out of the oven; in fact it is almost better cold than when it is hot.

This quantity of pastry is about a third more than is required for the case, but it is easier to roll out when there is some to spare.

Pastry

8oz/225g plain flour	*5oz/140g unsalted butter*
salt	*1 egg yolk (size 2)*

1¹/₂lb/675g courgettes	*1 egg yolk (size 2)*
1¹/₄oz/40g unsalted butter	*7fl oz/200ml double cream*
salt, pepper	*freshly grated nutmeg*
2 eggs (size 2)	

To make the pastry place the flour, salt and butter in the bowl of a food processor and reduce to a crumb-like consistency. Add the egg yolk and sufficient water to bring it together. Wrap this in clingfilm and chill it for 1 hour.

Preheat the oven to 180°C/350°F/Gas 4. Roll the pastry ⅛ inch/0.25cm thick on a lightly floured worksurface and line a 9 inch/22cm tart case 1½ inches/4cm deep with a removable base, allowing ¼ inch/0.5cm for shrinkage. Line this with foil and baking beans and bake for 15 minutes. Remove the foil and bake for a further 10 minutes until lightly coloured.

Cut the ends off the courgettes and slice thinly. Melt a knob of the butter in a frying pan, add some of the courgette slices, season and cook for several minutes, ensuring they do not colour. The slices should retain some of their body, and not become flaccid. Reserve the cooked courgette in a bowl. If it gives out juices this is perfectly all right – just let them mix with the custard mixture in the next stage.

Turn the oven up to 190°C/375°F/Gas 5. Whisk together the eggs, egg yolk and cream, and season with salt, pepper and nutmeg. Mix half of the custard with the courgettes. Lay the courgette slices in the tart case, arranging the surface layer neatly into concentric circles. Pour the remaining custard over and bake in the oven for 25 minutes.

Celery Tart with Saffron

When I first made this tart, it was by way of experimenting with saffron. The creamy celery flavoured with saffron needed some acidity and a stronger element to offset it. I hesitated about sprinkling the surface with Gruyère and was quite taken aback at the success of the combination.

Pastry

8oz/225g plain flour	*5oz/140g unsalted butter*
salt	*1 egg (size 2)*

1¼lb/550g celery stalks	*15 saffron filaments*
1oz/30g unsalted butter	*3fl oz/85ml vegetable stock*
4fl oz/115ml white wine	*1 level teaspoon cornflour blended*
7fl oz/200ml double cream	*with 1 tablespoon water*
salt, pepper	*4oz/115g Gruyère, grated*

To prepare the pastry, place the flour, salt and butter in the bowl of a food processor and reduce it to crumbs. Bring the dough together with the egg. Wrap the pastry in clingfilm and rest in the fridge for 1 hour.

Preheat the oven to 180°C/350°F/Gas 4. On a lightly floured surface roll the pastry ⅛ inch/0.25cm thick and line a shallow 9 inch/22cm tart tin with a removable base allowing ¼ inch/0.5cm for shrinkage – about a third of the pastry will be excess. Line with foil and baking beans and bake the case for 15 minutes. Remove the foil and beans and return it to the oven for a further 8 minutes until it is starting to turn golden.

While the pastry is resting prepare the filling. Peel the celery stalks with a potato peeler to remove the strings and cut it into ¼ inch/0.5cm slices. Melt the butter in a frying pan and sweat the celery for 5 minutes. Add the wine and cream, season and cook over a gentle heat for 10 minutes.

Toast the saffron in a dry frying pan for 1 minute, then grind it in a pestle and mortar. Heat the stock and infuse this with the saffron for 10 minutes. Add this tincture to the celery, with the cornflour solution, and cook for a further 5 minutes until the celery is coated in a rich sauce. Place this in the tart case and scatter the Gruyère over. Bake the tart for 25 minutes.

Koulibiaca with a Herb Sauce

A koulibiaca, also spelt with a 'c', without the final 'a' or 'kulebyaka', is the famous Russian fish pie, which to be truly authentic includes the dried spinal cord, the vesiga, of the sturgeon. For myself this is the stuff nightmares are made of, so no attempt has been made to replicate it. But the principle of a koulibiaca can be moulded with vegetarian ingredients retaining most of its original features. Authentically the recipe should use a brioche dough, but I find this too heavy and prefer puff pastry, which also takes a fraction of the time. However, I have included instructions for making brioche crust on page 161, should you want to.

This is a good centrepiece dish for a party. The filling is layered, so that when you slice the pie there is a base of wild rice with almonds and pine nuts, then a layer of carrots with dill, then mushroom duxelles and the compulsory sliced boiled eggs on top of this. Serve it with the herb sauce.

Rice layer

1oz/30g *wild rice*	³/₄oz/20g *flaked almonds*
2oz/55g *white rice*	3 *dessertspoons hazelnut oil*
³/₄oz/20g *pine nuts*	*salt, pepper*

Carrot layer

1lb/450g *carrots*	¹/₂ *teaspoon caster sugar*
³/₄oz/20g *unsalted butter*	1 *dessertspoon dill, finely chopped*
salt, pepper	

Mushroom layer

1¹/₄lb/550g *mushrooms*	*salt, pepper*
2 *shallots*	2 *heaped tablespoons parsley,*
1oz/30g *unsalted butter*	*finely chopped*

3 *eggs (size 2)*	1 *egg (size 2), beaten with*
1lb/450g *puff pastry*	1 *tablespoon water*

To prepare the rice layer, boil the wild rice in salted water for 40-45 minutes. Strain and reserve it. Cook the white rice for 15 minutes in salted water, strain and mix it with the wild rice. Toast the pine nuts and flaked almonds in the oven for 7-8 minutes at 180°/350°F/Gas 4. Add these to the rice, mix in the nut oil and season. Cover and keep in the fridge until required.

To make the carrot layer, peel the carrots and thinly slice them. Melt the butter in a frying pan, add the carrots, season with salt, pepper and the sugar and cook them for 12-15 minutes over a gentle heat so they are cooked but not coloured. Reserve in a bowl and mix in the dill.

Wipe the mushrooms and finely chop them in a food processor; do this in two lots to avoid reducing them to a complete mush. Finely chop the shallots also. Melt the butter in a frying pan and cook the mushrooms together with the shallots until the mixture is dry and pieces of mushroom begin to separate, approximately 15 minutes. Season it and stir in the parsley.

Boil the eggs for 10 minutes. Reserve in cold water and when they are cool, peel and slice them discarding the end of white.

Preheat the oven to 190°C/375°F/Gas 5. Halve the pastry and starting with one half, roll it on a lightly floured surface so it roughly forms a rectangle 12 x 8 inches/30 x 20cm. Lay this on a baking tray. Place the rice on the base leaving a good inch around it; it should form a strip about 5 inches/12cm wide. Place the carrots on top of this, then the mushroom mixture, and finally the eggs – it will now be about 4 inches/10cm tall. Paint the perimeter with the egg wash. Roll the second half of pastry so it will fit over the filling and lay this over. Trim the two edges leaving ³⁄₄ inch/1.5cm of spare pastry and fork this. Paint the surface lightly with the egg wash and bake it for 25 minutes until it is golden. It should not overcook or the pastry will dry out. Serve in slices with the sauce spooned over.

Brioche Dough

12oz/340g strong white flour	*4 eggs (size 2)*
1 level teaspoon salt	*6oz/170g unsalted butter*
1 sachet dried yeast or equivalent to ¹⁄₂oz/15g fresh	

To prepare the dough, warm the flour in the oven for a minute or two. Place this with the salt and yeast in the bowl of a food processor. Add the eggs and knead the dough for 5 minutes. Incorporate the softened butter. Place the dough, which will be sticky, in a bowl, cover it with a cloth or plastic bag, and allow it to rise to treble its volume in a warm place (75°F), which will take several hours.

Punch the dough down, without kneading it a great deal, and leave it in a cold place, loosely covered, for several hours. Bring it back to room temperature before it is required. Assemble the koulibiaca as described above.

Herb Sauce

1oz/30g *unsalted butter*
2 *shallots, finely chopped*
1 *dessertspoon each of chervil and*
  parsley, finely chopped
1 *teaspoon tarragon, finely chopped*
3fl oz/85ml *white wine*

$^1/_2$ pint/300ml *double cream*
$^1/_2$ pint/300ml *vegetable stock*
  reduced to 2fl oz
$^1/_2$ *teaspoon Dijon mustard*
salt, pepper
1 *egg yolk (size 2)*

Melt the butter and sweat the shallots for 2 minutes, then add the herbs and cook a moment longer. Add the wine and simmer for 1-2 minutes, then add the cream, stock, mustard and seasoning and cook for 4 minutes. Blend a little sauce with the egg yolk, return to the pan, and it should thicken instantly with the heat of the sauce. This sauce is rich and a little goes a long way.

Tomato and Basil Tart

This tart is light and elegant. Either make four 6 inch/15cm tarts or six 4 inch/10cm tarts. The tomato is layered on to puff pastry, so it is open-faced, pizza-fashion, but much lighter. Use small tomatoes, rather than the marmande, for slicing. Serve the tart about 15 minutes out of the oven; it is also pleasant when it is cold.

Season the tomato purée to taste; it may require more or less sugar depending on the sweetness of the tomatoes.

Purée

1lb/450g tomatoes	*1 level teaspoon caster sugar*
1 garlic clove	*salt, pepper*
1 dessertspoon arachide oil	*¹/₂ teaspoon thyme*
1 dessertspoon tomato purée	

1¹/₄lb/550g tomatoes	*¹/₄oz/7g basil*
1lb/450g puff pastry	*2 tablespoons extra virgin olive oil*
salt, pepper, caster sugar	*shavings of Parmesan*
¹/₂oz/15g unsalted butter	
1 egg (size 2), beaten with	
1 tablespoon water	

First of all skin all the tomatoes, both for the purée and the layer above, by immersing them in boiling water for 30 seconds and then in cold water. Deseed 1lb/450g of the skinned tomatoes; coarsely chop these for the purée. Slice the remainder, adding the top and bottom slices to the chopped tomato.

To prepare the purée, finely slice the garlic. Heat the oil in a small saucepan, add the garlic, and as soon as it gives off its aroma add the chopped tomato, the purée, sugar, seasoning and thyme. Cook this, stirring often, until it reduces to a thick, dry purée, which will take approximately 12 minutes.

Preheat the oven to 200°C/400°F/Gas 6. Roll the pastry thinly and cut out circles either 6 inches/15cm or 4 inches/10cm (see above). Divide the purée between them and spread it to within $\frac{1}{2}$ inch/1cm of the pastry rim. Next arrange a layer of tomato slices in concentric circles on top of the purée. Season with salt, pepper and sugar and dot with the butter. Paint the exposed rim of each tart with the beaten egg and bake them for 20 minutes.

Prepare a chiffonade of the basil and place this in the 2 tablespoons of olive oil. Just before serving, spread some of the basil on each tart with a few shavings of Parmesan in the centre (you may not require all the basil).

Spring Rolls with a Tomato, Ginger and Garlic Sauce

Usually spring rolls will contain cellophane noodles, maybe some Chinese mushrooms, pork and shrimps. The beauty of this filling is that the vegetables are cooked briefly in the wok, seared so as to retain all their natural flavour and some texture, and the end result is a lovely combination of delicate vegetable flavours.

I prefer to use filo pastry, which gives a lighter and crisper shell to a spring roll than a traditional wrapper.

6oz/170g *carrots, peeled*
7oz/200g *celeriac, trimmed weight*
4oz/115g *mangetouts*
4 *spring onions*
arachide oil
1 *teaspoon sesame oil*
8oz/225g *beansprouts*
1 *dessertspoon dry sherry*
light soy sauce

salt
1 *tablespoon white sesame seeds,*
    toasted for 2 minutes in a dry
    frying pan
8 *spring roll wrappers*
    8 *inches/20cm square, or*
    equivalent amount of filo pastry
egg white

Prepare a julienne of the carrots, celeriac and mangetouts. Trim and slice the spring onions. Heat 2 tablespoons of arachide oil with the sesame oil in a wok, and when it smokes throw in the carrot and celeriac. Keep these moving for 2 minutes, then add the mangetouts and onions and cook for 30 seconds, then the beansprouts and cook for a further 30 seconds. Add the sherry and let it vaporize, and season with the soy sauce and salt. Stir in the sesame seeds. Reserve this filling and allow to cool.

Place 2 tablespoons of the vegetable mixture on the corner of one spring roll wrapper, and roll inwards towards the opposite corner, tucking the sides in about half-way across. Moisten the end tip with egg white to secure it. Repeat with the rest of the filling – you should end up with approximately 8 rolls.

Heat plenty of arachide oil in a wok. When it is hot enough to make a cube of bread brown and crisp in a minute, add the spring rolls 4 at a time and cook for 5 minutes until golden and crisp on all sides. Drain on kitchen paper. They can be given a second frying, and prepared in advance if you wish, but slightly undercook first time round.

Tomato, Ginger and Garlic Sauce

This sauce is chunky, like a cooked salsa, vibrant with the flavours of ginger, garlic and coriander. Prepare it in advance of the spring rolls, then reheat it and whisk in the butter and herbs when you come to serve them.

---

1 tablespoon extra virgin olive oil
2 shallots, finely diced
1 heaped teaspoon fresh ginger, minced
2 garlic cloves, minced
2fl oz/55ml white wine
3 tablespoons passata
2 marmande tomatoes, peeled, seeded and diced

¹/₄ teaspoon chilli, finely diced
¹/₂ teaspoon caster sugar
salt, pepper
1oz/30g unsalted butter
1 dessertspoon coriander, chopped
chiffonade of 2 basil leaves

Heat the oil in a small saucepan, add the shallots, ginger and garlic and cook until soft. Add the white wine, passata, tomatoes, chilli, sugar and seasoning, bring to the boil and simmer for 10 minutes over a very low heat.

Just before serving the sauce, reheat it and whisk in the butter and the herbs.

See also:
Pissaladière (page 111)
Aubergine and Goat's Cheese Pizza with Roasted Garlic (page 113)
Calzone with Leeks, Thyme and Provolone (page 115)
Calzone with Broccoli and Gorgonzola (page 117)
Empanada with Caramelized Onions, Cabbage and Chestnuts, with a Butter Sauce (page 119)

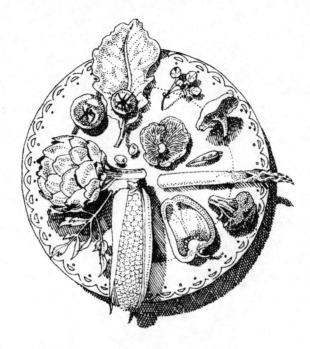

Hot and Cold
Vegetable Dishes

Sicilian Cauliflower

This robust treatment of cauliflower perfectly mirrors its rough texture and coarse flavour. The dish possesses an uncanny 'gamey' quality; it is quite assertive and likely to overpower any neighbouring dishes, so serve it by itself.

Perhaps, like myself, you will have returned from a trip to Sicily, mourning the fact that you are unable to find Caciocavallo here. This cheese literally translates as 'horse-cheese' and finds its way into any number of dishes in Sicily. It can be eaten fresh or aged up to 6 months, when it will be suitable for grating. The flavour of fresh Caciocavallo is mellow and it melts beautifully, making it a good cooking cheese. There is a Sicilian Caciocavallo which is the same as Provolone, and I now use this whenever I might want some Caciocavallo – it makes a perfectly good substitute.

Croûtons

3 slices white bread	*olive oil*

2 large cauliflowers	*1 teaspoon chilli, finely*
1 large garlic clove	*chopped*
1 onion	*3oz/85g Provolone, grated*
5oz/150ml black olives, stoned	*salt, pepper*
6fl oz/175ml red wine	*2 tablespoons flat-leaf parsley,*
3fl oz/85ml extra virgin olive oil	*finely chopped*
3 heaped teaspoons finely chopped	
sun-dried tomatoes	

Cut the crusts off the bread and cut into croûtons ¼ inch/0.5cm square. Heat a few millimetres of olive oil in a frying pan. When a cube of bread added to the oil is surrounded by bubbles, then it is sufficiently hot; fry the croûtons until they are crisp and uniformly golden. Drain and cool them on kitchen paper and reserve in a bowl.

Cut the cauliflowers into small florets. Mince the garlic, chop the onion and slice the olives. Coat the base of a heavy-bottomed saucepan with half each of the wine and olive oil, stir in the sun-dried tomatoes and arrange half the cauliflower over. Scatter over half the garlic, onion, olives, chilli and Provolone. Repeat these layers with the remainder of the ingredients. Bring to the boil, cover the saucepan with a tightly-fitting lid, and sweat for 10 minutes over a medium-low heat, stirring once. When the cauliflower is cooked, adjust the seasoning, stir in the parsley and serve with the croûtons alongside.

Vegetable Bourride

Traditionally a bourride is made with white fish, but happily the principle can be applied to a selection of vegetables. It lies half-way between a soup and a stew and is a glorious celebration of garlic: thickened with a garlic mayonnaise and served with garlic croûtons and lots of boiled potatoes to mop up the liquor. The selection of vegetables suggested is a 'theme on green' – it goes without saying that you should use what is seasonal and what is available.

Scorzonera, or black salsify, is a good inclusion if you can find it, in which case omit the courgettes. Prepare 8oz/225g of scorzonera as in the recipe for scorzonera croustades on page 129, then cook with the first lot of vegetables. Wearing rubber gloves to avoid staining your hands, peel the scorzonera and cut it into 3 inch/7.5cm lengths. If there is any delay in placing the scorzonera in the cooking liquor, reserve it in a bowl of acidulated water.

You may find it easier to serve this in shallow soup bowls rather than on dinner plates.

Garlic mayonnaise

---

8 garlic cloves	10fl oz/275ml extra virgin olive
salt	oil
2 egg yolks (size 2)	lemon juice
3/4 teaspoon Dijon mustard	

pinch saffron filaments	2lb/900g potatoes, peeled
5 shallots	8oz/225g broccoli
2 large leeks	8oz/225g courgettes
8oz/225g small kohl rabi	8oz/225g green beans
1 pint/600ml vegetable stock	8oz/225g broad beans, skinned
5fl oz/150ml white wine	2 heaped tablespoons flat-leaf
salt, pepper	parsley leaves

Croûtons

¹/₂ loaf French bread	1 garlic clove
extra virgin olive oil	

To prepare the garlic mayonnaise, peel and roughly chop the garlic cloves. Sprinkle some salt over them and using the flat edge of a knife crush to a paste, mincing and crushing until it is fine. Whisk the garlic with the egg yolks and mustard. Slowly dribble in the oil, whisking constantly. The mayonnaise should reach a point where the egg yolks are saturated with oil and it is too thick to whisk; add more than the 10fl oz/275ml of oil if necessary. Squeeze in a little lemon juice.

Toast the saffron in a dry frying pan for 1 minute until it is brittle, then grind in a pestle and mortar and infuse with 1 tablespoon boiling water for 10 minutes.

Peel the shallots. Trim the leeks, removing the outer, tough layers, quarter them lengthwise and cut into 3 inch/7.5cm lengths. Peel the kohl rabi and quarter. Place the vegetable stock, wine and seasoning in a saucepan and bring to a simmer. Place these vegetables into the cooking liquor, cover the pan and simmer for 10 minutes.

Bring a large pan of salted water to the boil and put the potatoes on to cook.

Cut the broccoli into florets, quarter the courgettes lengthwise and cut into batons 3 inches/7.5cm long, top and tail the beans. Add these and the broad beans to the stew and cook covered for another 15 minutes in total, adding the saffron tincture and the parsley leaves 5 minutes before the end. The liquor will by no means cover the vegetables; they will steam.

While the stew is cooking prepare the croûtons. Slice the French bread ½ inch/1cm thick, heat a couple of tablespoons of olive oil in a frying pan and fry the bread on both sides until it is crisp in patches, adding more oil as necessary. It should be more like traditional British fried bread than the crisp croûtons of French cuisine. Rub one surface with garlic.

When the vegetables are cooked remove them with a slotted spoon to a large and shallow serving dish. Incorporate a little of the cooking liquor into the mayonnaise and return this to the pan. Cook over a low heat until it thickens into a thin sauce without it boiling, and adjust the seasoning. Strain it over the vegetables. Accompany the bourride with the fried bread and boiled potatoes.

Ratatouille with Samphire Fritters

Samphire comes in saline contrast to the sweetness of the ratatouille. The batter is the consistency of a pancake batter, and fritters form instantly as spoonfuls of the samphire batter are dropped into the hot oil. My mother, I suspect like many cooks of her generation, fell victim to an early design of deep-fat fryer: I was raised on the horror story of how once, while deep-frying, she left the kitchen for a few minutes and was recalled to it by clouds of black smoke billowing from the doorway. She spent a happy summer repainting the entire house. This together with tales of pressure cookers blowing up are firmly ingrained in my cookery psyche, and I have never acquired either gadget. A wok is perfect for deep-frying and worth keeping specifically for that. Even if you never use it for anything else, it saves wrecking your best stainless steel saucepans with indelible and sticky oil stains. You can always use a thermometer to check the temperature if you are unsure.

While ratatouille can be eaten hot or cold, the flavours are best at room temperature. Too often ratatouille is stewed to a homogeneous and rather slimy mush. The method used here leaves each vegetable intact, coated in a richly flavoured sauce. The ratatouille should be prepared in advance. The fritters can be prepared in advance to the stage indicated in the recipe, but they must be eaten as soon as they are cooked.

1lb/450g aubergines	*bouquet garni (see page seven)*
salt	*1 teaspoon balsamic vinegar or*
1 onion	*aged red wine vinegar*
extra virgin olive oil	*salt, pepper*
3 garlic cloves, crushed to a paste	*1lb/450g courgettes*
with salt	*2 red peppers*
2lb/900g marmande tomatoes,	*2 tablespoons parsley,*
peeled, seeded and chopped	*finely chopped*
2 teaspoons tomato purée	*small handful of basil*

Slice the aubergines ½ inch/1cm thick and quarter each slice. Sprinkle with salt and leave them to exude their juices in a colander for 30 minutes.

Peel and slice the onion into rings and separate these. Heat 2 tablespoons of olive oil in a small saucepan. Cook the onion for a couple of minutes, add the garlic and cook a minute longer. Add the tomatoes, the purée, and the bouquet garni. Cover the pan and cook the sauce over a low heat for 20 minutes, stirring it occasionally. Discard the herbs and stir in the balsamic vinegar and seasoning.

Rinse and pat dry the aubergine. Heat 3 tablespoons of oil in a frying pan, add all the aubergine and cook for 10 minutes over a medium heat. Transfer it to a casserole with a lid.

Slice the courgettes ¼ inch/0.5cm thick. Heat a couple of tablespoons of oil in the frying pan and cook for 6 minutes. Add it to the aubergine.

Peel the peppers using a potato peeler, and remove the core and inner membranes and seeds. Cut them into strips. Add more oil to the pan if necessary and cook these for 8 minutes. Add them to the other vegetables.

Preheat the oven to 180°C/350°F/Gas 4. Pour the sauce over the vegetables and mix. Cover the casserole and cook the ratatouille for 15 minutes in the oven. Check it to see if it is cooked; the vegetables should be just done – if not, give them a little longer. Once it has cooled, adjust the seasoning and gently stir in the chopped parsley. Scatter a few leaves of torn basil over just before serving.

Samphire fritters

7oz/200g samphire	*3¹/₂fl oz/100ml water*
1 egg (size 2)	*pinch salt*
2oz/55g plain flour	*arachide oil for deep-frying*
1 tablespoon olive oil	*lemon wedges to serve*

Pick over the samphire, discarding any tough stems and discoloured or slimy shoots. Wash it well, and dry it carefully.

Separate the egg, reserve the egg white, and whisk the yolk with the flour, oil, water and salt into a smooth paste. The recipe can be prepared in advance to this stage.

Just before frying the fritters, whisk the egg white until it is stiff and fold it into the batter, then mix in the samphire. The samphire should be well-coated in batter with a little extra, but not swamped.

Heat plenty of oil in a wok, or pan, to 180°C/350°F. Drop teaspoons of the fritter mixture into the oil (half a dessertspoon may be easier) and cook them to a golden brown, turning them as necessary. Remove the fritters with a slotted spoon and drain on kitchen paper. Provide lemon wedges separately, and squeeze over a few drops of juice immediately before eating the fritters.

Courgette Flowers stuffed with Mozzarella, Tomato and Basil

This dish is easy to prepare, delightful as a starter or as an accompaniment to other dishes such as the courgette tart on page 155. Both male and female flowers can be eaten, but it is the female flower which produces the courgette and is called for in this recipe.

6 *female courgette flowers, with courgette*	*salt*
2 *eggs (size 2)*	*vegetable oil for deep-frying*
1 *dessertspoon double cream*	*plain flour*

Filling

5oz/140g *buffalo mozzarella*	1 *garlic clove, crushed*
2oz/55g *tomato, skinned, seeded and diced*	1 *tablespoon freshly grated Parmesan*
1 *teaspoon basil, finely chopped*	*salt, pepper*
2 *teaspoons flat-leaf parsley, finely chopped*	

Trim the base of each courgette and gently prise apart the petals of the flower.

To make the filling, first grate or chop the mozzarella. Combine this in a bowl with the remaining ingredients for the filling and stuff the flower cavities, packing it down firmly. Leave enough space to twist the petals together at the top.

Beat the eggs with the cream and season with salt. Heat plenty of oil in a large pan or a wok. Roll each courgette in flour, then dip lightly into the egg. Fry until the flowers turn a light golden – the courgette need not be well cooked. The mozzarella melts almost immediately. Drain on kitchen paper and serve.

Celeriac Purée with Fried Parsley

Passed through a mouli-légumes, this purée retains some texture. It is served with a surround of crisp, deep-fried parsley and some thin toast. Serve it as a starter, or without trimmings as a more conventional accompaniment to a main dish. The purée and croûtons can be made in advance, the herbs fried at the last minute.

Croûtons

4 thin slices white bread	1¹/₂oz/45g unsalted butter, clarified

Purée

juice of ¹/₂ lemon	3fl oz/85ml milk
3lb/1.4kg celeriac	freshly grated nutmeg
(2 average-sized roots)	salt, white pepper
5fl oz/150ml crème fraîche	

Fried parsley

1¹/₂oz/45g curly parsley	vegetable oil for deep-frying

To prepare the croûtons, preheat the oven to 180°C/350°F/Gas 4. Remove the crusts from the bread and cut into triangles. Lay them on a baking sheet and place in the oven for 4-5 minutes until they dry out. Paint them with the melted, clarified butter. Return to the oven for 10-12 minutes or until they turn golden. Cool on parchment paper before stacking.

To prepare the purée, bring a large pan of water to the boil and acidulate it with the lemon juice. Cut the skin from the celeriac roots and cut them into pieces. Boil for 10 minutes, then drain and pass through a mouli-légumes. Stir in the crème fraîche and milk, and season with nutmeg, salt and pepper.

Pick over the parsley, discarding the stalks. Heat the oil and deep-fry it, which will only take a matter of seconds – the oil must be hot but not so hot that it singes the parsley. Drain it on kitchen paper.

Serve the hot purée with the parsley scattered around it, accompanied by the croûtons.

Beetroot Purée with Fried Sorrel and Parsley

This is a variation on the above theme. A rich, bright vermilion, with a surround of crisp green parsley and ethereal sheaths of sorrel: perfect Christmas food. It is an elegant accompaniment to any festive dish, and more exciting than boiled veg; otherwise serve it as a starter with some triangles of finely sliced rye or walnut bread, baked to a golden crispness in the oven.

2lb/900g beetroot	*1 teaspoon balsamic vinegar*
8oz/225g parsnip	*lemon juice*
½ cooking apple	*salt, pepper*
5fl oz/150ml sour cream	

Fried herbs

vegetable oil for deep-frying	*³/₄oz/20g sorrel leaves*
³/₄oz/20g curly parsley, without tough stalks	

Preheat the oven to 160°C/325°F/Gas 2. Wash the beetroots carefully, place in a baking dish and cover with foil. Cook for 3 hours, then skin them and reduce to a coarse purée in a food processor.

Peel the parsnip and apple and cut into ½ inch/1cm cubes. Steam the parsnip for 10 minutes and the apple for 3-4 minutes. Purée the beetroot, parsnip and apple with the sour cream in a liquidizer until smooth. Add the vinegar, a few drops of lemon juice and seasoning. The purée can be made in advance; reheat to serve, but if you are using a good balsamic vinegar than add it at the end.

Heat the oil; it should not be too hot. Deep-fry the herbs for a matter of seconds then drain on kitchen paper. The parsley should retain its colour, the sorrel will turn a dull green.

Serve the hot beetroot purée with the herbs scattered over it.

Char-grilled Aubergine and Salsa on Fried Bread

There is a rich vulgarity about this salsa, the loud exclamation of raw onion, lime juice, chilli and coriander jostling together.

Salsa

2 marmande tomatoes	*3/4 teaspoon chilli, finely diced*
1 large red pepper	*salt*
2 shallots, minced	*2 level tablespoons coriander,*
juice of 1/2 lime	*finely chopped*
3 tablespoons extra virgin olive oil	

2 aubergines	*salt, pepper*
extra virgin olive oil	*4-6 slices day-old white bread*

Make the salsa as close to the time of serving as possible. Skin, deseed and dice the tomatoes and place in a bowl. Peel and deseed the pepper, dice the same size as the tomato, and add to the bowl. Add all the remaining salsa ingredients.

To cook the aubergines, slice 1/2 inch/1cm thick, cutting on the bias. Heat the griddle, brush one side of each aubergine slice with olive oil and grill for 3-4 minutes until it is streaked with dark brown. Paint the top side with olive oil, season and turn the slices over, and give another 3-4 minutes.

While the aubergine is cooking, fry the bread. Heat a couple of tablespoons of olive oil in a frying pan and cook the bread on both sides until golden and brown. Serve the aubergine slices on the fried bread with a heap of salsa on top.

Tomatoes stuffed with Celeriac-Rémoulade with a Parsley Vinaigrette

When I think of celeriac, I think of celeriac-rémoulade: a salad of blanched celeriac mixed with a mustard-flavoured mayonnaise, sometimes with the addition of parsley, which is present here in the vinaigrette, and occasionally garlic. The most time-consuming part of the recipe is making a julienne of the celeriac. It could also be grated – the coarse-grating blade of a food processor would make light work of this. This quantity is sufficient to stuff 6 small tomatoes or 4 large ones.

4 large or 6 small marmande tomatoes, firm but ripe	salt, pepper

Rémoulade

juice of 1 lemon	1 heaped teaspoon Dijon mustard
1½lb/675g celeriac	7fl oz/200ml arachide oil
1 egg yolk (size 2)	salt

Parsley vinaigrette

1 tablespoon sherry vinegar	2 heaped tablespoons flat-leaf
salt, pepper	parsley, finely chopped
7 tablespoons extra virgin olive oil	

Bring a pan of water to the boil and fill the sink with cold water. Plunge the tomatoes into the boiling water for 30 seconds then immediately into the cold water. When they are cool, skin them, slice off and discard the top of each tomato, and scoop out the inside; the bulk can be cut out, but a melon-baller or a teaspoon will assist in tidying it up.

Juice the lemon. Place half the juice in a bowl of cold water and the other half in a saucepan of salted water; bring this to the boil. Cut the skin from the celeriac and slice it thinly about ⅛ inch/0.25cm thick; make a julienne of strips 1 inch/2cm long and reserve them in the acidulated cold water. Strain the celeriac and cook it in the boiling water for 2½ minutes, using a slotted spoon to remove it to a sink of cold water.

To prepare the mayonnaise, whisk together the egg yolk and the mustard, gradually whisk in the oil and season with salt. Dry the celeriac thoroughly between two tea towels and mix it with this sauce.

To make the vinaigrette, whisk the vinegar with ½ teaspoon salt and some pepper until the salt dissolves. Add the olive oil and the chopped parsley.

The dish can be prepared in advance to this point. To serve it, season the inside of the tomatoes with salt and pepper and fill each cavity until it is piled high with the rémoulade. Spoon some of the vinaigrette to the side of each tomato.

Guacamole with Potato Crisps

Avocados are rich and creamy and at their best with a sharp dressing to balance this. This version of guacamole is flavoured with lime juice, coriander, spring onions and chillis, with the added advantage that the lime juice will prevent the avocado from discolouring for several hours.

The potato crisps are baked in the oven. They are well-flavoured and rustic, though not as rich as the very thin and ethereal deep-fried crisps. Blue corn chips, available from healthfood outlets, are also a good accompaniment, or you could resort to Kettle Chips.

---

1 marmande tomato
4 ripe Hass avocados
juice of 1 lime
2 tablespoons extra virgin olive oil
1 tablespoon coriander, finely
  chopped

1 tablespoon spring onion, finely
  sliced
1 teaspoon green chilli, finely
  chopped
salt

Skin and deseed the tomato and dice it into ¼ inch/0.5cm cubes. Dice the avocado flesh a similar size. Place these together in a bowl, add the lime juice and olive oil and toss lightly, then very gently fold in the coriander, spring onion and chilli and season with salt. Care must be taken not to over-stir the guacamole, hence mashing the avocado.

Potato Crisps

1½ lb/675g potatoes
extra virgin olive oil

salt

Preheat the oven to 200°C/400°F/Gas 6. Peel the potatoes and finely slice them; a mandolin will assist here. Rinse the potato slices, blanch them in boiling salted water for 1 minute, drain and pat them dry.

Brush several baking sheets with olive oil and lay out the slices, which should not overlap. Trickle over a little olive oil and sprinkle with salt. Bake these until they are golden. They never bake at an even rate – the first ones may be done after 10 minutes, the thicker ones are likely to take 20 minutes.

Cool them on a rack until they are crisp and eat them as soon as possible.

Globe Artichokes with a Balsamic Vinaigrette

When an artichoke is presented whole, leaves and choke intact, eating it can be rather laborious. Sucking on a hundred leaves in order to reach the good bit underneath almost feels like a punishment. In this recipe the best of the leaves are served beside the artichoke heart, which effectively means having the good bits without all the work.

There are many ways of stuffing artichoke hearts, but little suits them better than if they are boiled and eaten with a simple vinaigrette. Artichokes cry out for vinegar or lemon juice so the vinaigrette needs to be sharp, and since it plays such an important role, the olive oil used should be a very good one.

To garnish

2 eggs

---

4 large globe artichokes	*juice of 3 lemons*

Dressing

---

1 tablespoon balsamic vinegar	*8 tablespoons extra virgin olive oil*
salt, pepper	*1 shallot, finely chopped*

First prepare the garnish: hard-boil the eggs for 10 minutes. Cool in cold water, then shell them and separate the yolks from the whites. Finely chop the white and press the yolk through a sieve; reserve these separately.

To prepare the artichokes, bring a large pan of water to the boil and add two-thirds of the lemon juice. Use the remainder of the juice for dipping the artichoke as you expose the flesh. To pare the artichoke, break off the stalk from each one and cut away the base, removing all the tough green parts. Cut around the sides so as to remove the tough outer layer of leaves, leaving the rest of the leaves and the choke intact. Cook these for 20 minutes. Reserve in cold water until required.

To make the vinaigrette, whisk the vinegar with the seasoning and add the olive oil and the chopped shallot.

Squeeze the water from the leaves and drain the artichoke on kitchen paper. Pull off any loose outer leaves, or tough-looking ones. Holding the artichoke heart, pull off the leaves so they remain intact as a cone; do this by working around the choke to loosen them where they join the heart. Pull out the centre leaves from the cone, including any thin purple and white leaves, and discard these. With a knife cut out the choke and trim the edge, and with a teaspoon scrape off the pitted layer where the choke was rooted to the heart.

To serve, place a heart on each plate and a cone of leaves beside it, spoon the vinaigrette over the heart and around it, and garnish with some of the chopped egg white and sieved yolk.

Potatoes and Gnocchi

Baked Potatoes

Scrub baking potatoes and dry them. Make an incision the shape of a lid on the top of each one with a small sharp knife. Place a little olive oil in the palm of your hand, rub your hands together and then over the potatoes, so coating each one lightly with the oil. Place them on a baking dish and sprinkle over some crystals of sea salt. Bake for $1^1/_2$ hours at 160°C/325°F/Gas 3.

Baked Potatoes filled with Fennel and Saffron

Sitting in front of a huge baked potato filled with creamy fennel and potato purée is heaven as an informal supper, but if you want to make the affair a little more elegant then serve 2 smaller potatoes per person and garnish the plate with herb fronds or watercress. Perhaps fill one potato as below, and another with the 'champ' of sweet potatoes, leeks and basil on page 206.

---

4 baking potatoes
extra virgin olive oil

crystalline sea salt

Filling

---

a large fennel bulb, or 2 small ones
3fl oz/85ml white wine
6fl oz/175ml double cream
salt, pepper

25 saffron filaments
1oz/30g sorrel
$^1/_2$oz/15g unsalted butter

For the potato purée

1fl oz/30ml double cream	*salt, pepper*
2fl oz/55ml extra virgin olive oil	

Bake the potatoes according to the method described above.

To prepare the fennel and saffron filling, first dice the fennel. The way of approaching this is not always obvious first time around: trim each bulb and discard the outer sheath, then halve the bulbs vertically, cutting through the shoots so that you have two flat halves. Place these cut side down on the chopping board and slice horizontally through the bulb, at ¼ inch/0.5cm thicknesses, stopping ½ inch/1cm from the root so that it remains held together. Make vertical incisions at ¼ inch/0.5cm spaces, again stopping ½ inch/1cm from the root. Now slice the fennel, working from the shoots to the root end, and it will fall into ¼ inch/0.5cm dice. In other words, exactly the same method you would use when chopping onions.

Place the fennel together with the wine, cream and seasoning in a small saucepan and cook over a gentle heat for 25-30 minutes, stirring occasionally. Roast the saffron in a dry frying pan for 1 minute, grind it in a pestle and mortar and pour over 1 tablespoon of boiling water; infuse for 10 minutes. Add the saffron tincture to the fennel 5 minutes before the end of cooking. The fennel should be soft, and coated in a rich, thick sauce.

Cut the sorrel into strips, heat the ½oz/15g of butter in a frying pan and sweat it for a minute or two until it wilts and changes colour to a dull green.

Remove the lid from each potato, reserving it, scoop out the inside of the potato to within ¼ inch/0.5cm of the skin and pass it through a sieve into a bowl. Blend the cream, olive oil and seasoning into the purée.

To assemble the potatoes, divide the sorrel between the cases, lining the base of each. Spoon the fennel on top of this and fill the remainder of the cavity with the potato purée, pressing it down firmly; replace the lids. The potatoes can be prepared to this point in advance and reheated for 20 minutes at 160°C/325°F/Gas 3 from cold.

Pommes Anna with Leeks and Provolone

Finely sliced potatoes are layered with leeks and cheese, which adhere together into a cake. Traditionally butter is added between each layer, which is unnecessary here due to the fat in the cheese. An omelette pan or small frying pan work perfectly, and the whole thing is inverted once cooked. Usually Pommes Anna will have a crisp exterior; accidentally, when I was trying to achieve this, I turned out a dish as soft on the outside as it was in the centre. As the dish, intended for 4, bit by bit disappeared into the mouths of 2, I decided it should stay this way.

1lb/450g leeks, trimmed weight	salt, pepper
1 garlic clove	1³/₄lb/800g potatoes
1³/₄oz/50g unsalted butter and	2oz/55g Provolone, grated
³/₄oz/20g to butter the pan	2oz/55g Gruyère, grated
1 teaspoon thyme	

Wash the leeks, halve them lengthwise and chop them, and mince the clove of garlic. Melt 1¹/₄oz/40g of the butter in a frying pan and cook the leeks, garlic, thyme and seasoning for 5 minutes until soft, though not coloured.

Preheat the oven to 190°C/375°F/Gas 5. Peel the potatoes and slice transparently thin, using a mandolin if you have one, discarding the end slices. Choose an 8 inch/20cm frying pan with a heat-resistant handle and place a square of foil on the base so that when the dish is turned out it does not stick. Butter the pan very well, using about ³/₄oz/20g butter. Lay a layer of potato slices in concentric circles on the base, starting with a circle in the centre and then working towards the outside. This layer should be quite thick. Sprinkle over a little salt, scatter over half of the leeks and half of the cheese. Repeat the layers until all the ingredients are used up: there should be 3 layers of potato, 2 of filling. Dot the surface with the remaining butter and cover with foil. Bake this for 1 hour. Loosen the base using a flexible palette knife and invert it on to a plate.

Bubble and Squeak

As a child I remember the frying pan hissing with a cake of green cabbage and white potato, frequently turned as the underside became golden and crisp until it was green, white and golden in the right proportions. It was generally part of a brunch-time 'fry-up', and was pleasantly peppered up with a dash or two of Lea and Perrins.

This version is cooked traditionally in a frying pan on the stove top. Serve the bubble with a few drops of Tabasco; it can be accompanied by a poached egg and some wild mushrooms, or some other tasty variety of mushroom. Allow 1 egg per person, softly poach them according to the instructions on page 60, and fry 1lb/450g mushrooms in a little butter.

I have suggested kale be used. Its bitterness is partly offset by the red onions, and pleasantly tempered by the sweetness of the potatoes. Obviously any green cabbage can be used – turnip greens would also be excellent.

2lb/900g potatoes
7oz/200g kale, tough stalks
  removed
1 red onion

1¹/₄oz/40g *unsalted butter*
2 tablespoons olive oil
salt, pepper

Peel the potatoes and cook them in boiling salted water for 20 minutes until they are just cooked. Drain them and leave in a colander until the surface water evaporates, then chop coarsely.

Wash the kale, bring a large pan of salted water to the boil, add the kale and cook it for 2 minutes once it has come back to the boil. Drain thoroughly, pressing out the water, and chop it coarsely.

Peel, quarter and slice the onion. Heat ¹/₂oz/15g of the butter and 1 tablespoon of olive oil in a frying pan and cook the onion for 5 minutes; it should not colour. Add the kale, season with salt and pepper, and cook for a further 5 minutes.

Heat 1 tablespoon of olive oil and the remaining butter in a frying pan, sauté the potato until it turns crispy, about 20-25 minutes, and season it. Add the kale and cook for another few minutes.

Colcannon served with Shallots and Lentils Braised in Red Wine

Colcannon originates in Ireland, where it took the form of festival food, being eaten at Hallowe'en. A lucky charm was pushed into the mixture, either a ring, a button, a horseshoe, a thimble or a coin: the lucky recipient of the ring could expect to be married within the year.

A simple but inspired recipe of my mother's was to cook thinly shredded white cabbage in butter, seasoning it generously with freshly grated nutmeg, salt and pepper. Here I have cooked Savoy cabbage in this fashion; it is mixed with a purée of potatoes, then baked in the oven until you have a crisp shell filled with a silken purée of potatoes and cabbage.

I have suggested an accompaniment of shallots and lentils braised with red wine and thyme, but any wintry stew such as this can be served on a bed of bubble and squeak or colcannon.

3lb/1.4kg potatoes	*2oz/55g unsalted butter*
salt, pepper	*nutmeg*
1lb/450g Savoy cabbage	

Peel the potatoes and cook them in boiling, salted water for 20-25 minutes or until they are well cooked. Drain them and allow them to stand in the colander until they are dry and the surface steam has evaporated. Pass through a sieve or a mouli-légumes and season.

Shred the cabbage, cutting out the core and discarding any tough or thick parts. Melt half the butter in a saucepan and toss the cabbage in this, then add 5 tablespoons water, cover, and cook for 4 minutes over a low heat. It should be limp but not well cooked. Season it with freshly grated nutmeg, salt and pepper.

Preheat the oven to 200°C/400°F/Gas 6. Combine the potato purée and the cabbage. Butter a gratin dish which will hold the mixture to a depth of $1^{1}/_{2}$ inches/4cm. Press the mixture into this and fork the surface into furrows. Dot the remaining butter over the surface and bake for 30-35 minutes.

Shallots and Lentils Braised in Red Wine

2 level tablespoons Puy lentils	1 bay leaf
$^{1}/_{4}$oz/7g dried wild mushrooms	8fl oz/225ml red wine
1lb/450g shallots	1oz/30g unsalted butter
6oz/170g baby carrots	1 tablespoon olive oil
7 sprigs thyme	salt, pepper

Boil the lentils for 20 minutes, strain and reserve. Cover the dried wild mushrooms with 5fl oz/150ml boiling water and soak for 15 minutes. Peel the shallots, leaving them whole, likewise the baby carrots unless they are very 'baby', in which case just wash them and top and tail. Drain the mushrooms, reserving the liquor, and chop. Strain the liquor through a fine-mesh sieve or muslin if it appears gritty. Place all the ingredients in a saucepan, including the mushroom liquor, bring to the boil, cover with a lid, and braise over a gentle heat for 40 minutes.

Remove the sprigs of thyme and the bay leaf and serve this over the colcannon.

Champ

Maybe when Richard Dreyfuss forked his mashed potato into a table-top mountain in *Close Encounters of the Third Kind*, he was playing with a plate of champ, as it does lend itself to this sort of behaviour. Perhaps Irish children do the same, or use the eerie and isolated Mountains of Mourne as their model.

The puritan in me finds the prospect of devouring a mound of champ, wet with molten butter, a delightful but rather sinful prospect. This is irrational given the nature of many pasta dishes, which are equally brazen if not as bare-faced. Champ is a purée of potatoes mixed with spring onions or other greens and enriched with buttermilk. Once mounded, it is served with a generous knob of salted butter pushed into its crest. If buttermilk is unavailable, use 2 tablespoons of a natural live yoghurt. I have suggested watercress, which gives quite a dominant flavour; the nettles are more muted.

Champ finds a natural habitat inside the shell of a baked potato (keep the cooked inside of the potato for some other use). Bake the potatoes according to the instructions on page 195.

3lb/1.4kg potatoes
2 bunches spring onions
(approx 15)
2oz/55g watercress or nettle-tops

4fl oz/115ml double cream
salt, pepper
3 tablespoons buttermilk
1oz/30g salted butter

Peel the potatoes and cook them in boiling, salted water for 20 minutes until they are well cooked. Drain and leave them standing in a colander until any surface water has evaporated, then pass through a sieve or mouli-légumes.

Trim the spring onions, leaving most of the green part, and chop them. Wash and coarsely chop the watercress or nettles. Place the onions and greens in a small saucepan with the cream and seasoning. Cover the pan and cook over a gentle heat for 10 minutes, making sure it does not catch. The mixture should be quite dry, so if it is sauce-like cook it a minute or two longer with the lid off until it dries out.

Mix the cream and onion mixture and the buttermilk into the potato purée, adjusting the seasoning. Reheat it and serve either in bowls with a knob of butter bedded in the centre, or as suggested above inside a baked potato and garnish with a few sprigs of flat-leaf parsley or watercress.

'Champ' of Sweet Potatoes, Leeks and Basil

Sometimes I make this with sorrel instead of basil, or a combination could be used. Slice the basil just before it goes into the pan.

2lb/900g sweet potatoes	*salt, pepper*
3 tablespoons buttermilk	*2 tablespoons basil, cut into strips*
3 large leeks	*1¹/₂oz/45g salted butter*
3fl oz/85ml double cream	

Peel the sweet potatoes, cut them into even-sized pieces and cook them in boiling salted water for 10 minutes. Drain and allow them to steam in the colander until the surface water evaporates, then pass through a sieve or mouli-légumes. Stir in the buttermilk.

Wash the leeks, slit them lengthwise and slice them. Place them in a small saucepan with the cream and seasoning and cook, covered, over a gentle heat for 10 minutes. Add the basil and cook another 2 minutes. Combine this with the potato purée and adjust the seasoning. Reheat it and serve it either in bowls with a knob of butter bedded in the centre, or as suggested above inside a baked potato and garnished with a few sprigs of flat-leaf parsley or watercress.

Potato and Truffle Salad

I love food which combines simplicity with luxury, such as this salad. First procure your truffle, boil some good waxy new potatoes, slice them and trickle over the best olive oil you can find, scatter with slivers of truffle and consume.

2lb/900g new potatoes	*salt, pepper*
extra virgin olive oil	*1oz/40g Périgord truffle*

Select potatoes of the same size, peel them and boil them in salted water until cooked. Drain and cool for 5 minutes.

Slice the potatoes, discarding the end slices, and arrange on plates. Trickle over some olive oil and season. Finely shave the truffle and scatter it over the potato.

Saffron Potatoes

Dye potatoes a glorious sunshine yellow by boiling them in water containing saffron, or make an equally glorious mound of saffron mash by mixing cream infused with saffron into a potato purée. This is Raymond Blanc's *'pommes de terre aux pistils de safran'*, glazed and golden. Serve them as an accompaniment to any dish with Provençal characteristics.

---

15 saffron filaments, roasted and
   ground (see page 9)
3¹/₂fl oz/100ml vegetable stock
1¹/₄lb/550g new potatoes
³/₄oz/20g unsalted butter

2 shallots, finely chopped
1 sprig thyme
1 bay leaf
salt, black pepper

Cover the ground saffron with 1 tablespoon of boiling stock and leave for 10 minutes. Select potatoes of a similar size, peel and reserve in cold water. Heat the butter in a medium-sized saucepan and sweat the shallots and potatoes for a couple of minutes. Add the saffron, thyme, bay leaf and seasoning. Turn the potatoes until they are well coated in saffron. Add the stock and cover the potatoes with buttered paper, then the lid. Cook for 15 minutes, stirring once. The liquid should have evaporated.

Gnocchi

There are many variants of gnocchi, or dumplings, the most common being potato gnocchi. Then there are spinach and ricotta gnocchi, ones made with pumpkin, semolina and sweet versions also. The bullet-like dumplings which pose as gnocchi in vacuum-packed plastic are a poor recommendation for the genuine product. The battle is to create a dumpling that holds together without being tough in texture. When light and delicate they can be delectable.

When I first came to make gnocchi, I was usually confounded when it came to storing them. Either I would stack them in a bowl so that when it came to cooking them they had stuck together, resulting in an indelicate attempt to prise them apart, or they had squashed together into unseemly shapes. Gnocchi are designed to be eaten fresh, as soon after they are made as possible, but can be kept for a matter of hours if necessary. There are two ways of keeping them if they are not to be cooked immediately. Either lay a tea towel on a tray and dust it with flour, lay the gnocchi on this in a single layer so they are not touching and then lay another tea towel on top. Store in the fridge until required. Alternatively, blanch them for 30 seconds, then plunge into cold water, toss with olive oil and cook as usual when they are required. This method is often used in restaurants. In fact it takes only minutes to shape the gnocchi once the dough is made, and I think it is best, if time allows, to roll and cook them freshly.

Potato Gnocchi with Tomato and Basil Sauce

1lb 6oz/625g potatoes	*salt, pepper*
2 egg yolks (size 2)	*5oz/140g 'Farina 00'*
freshly grated nutmeg	*(see page 228)*

Boil the potatoes in their skins. When they are cool enough to handle, skin them and pass them through a sieve or mouli-légumes. Mix in the egg yolks and season with nutmeg, salt and pepper. Gradually work the flour into the potato. Do not mix more than is necessary – the dough will be sticky.

Flour a worksurface, take a lump of the mixture, and roll it into a long, thin sausage, no more than ½ inch/1cm in diameter. Slice this ¼ inch/0.5cm thick. Take a fork and run the tines over one of the cut sides of the gnocchi. This flattens the dumpling so that it cooks evenly and the ridges allow more sauce to be held. Store the gnocchi as recommended above.

To cook the gnocchi, bring a large pan of salted water to the boil. Add the gnocchi. They will rise to the surface after a minute or two; give them one minute longer, remove with a slotted spoon and toss with the sauce.

Tomato and Basil Sauce

2lb/900g *marmande tomatoes*	1 *level teaspoon caster sugar*
1¹/₂oz/45g *unsalted butter*	*salt, pepper*
1 *tablespoon olive oil*	*small handful of basil*

To prepare the tomato sauce, skin and deseed the tomatoes. Dice the flesh and place in a small saucepan with the butter, olive oil, sugar, salt and pepper. Cook this until it reduces by about half into a thick, textured sauce. Make a chiffonade of the basil and add to the sauce.

Potato Gnocchi with Gorgonzola

1 quantity of gnocchi (see above)

Sauce

5oz/140g Gorgonzola	*cayenne pepper*
4 tablespoons double cream	*1 marmande tomato, peeled, seeded*
1oz/30g unsalted butter	*and diced*

Prepare the gnocchi as indicated above.

Break up the Gorgonzola and place together with the cream, butter and cayenne pepper in a small saucepan. Heat and blend together with a wooden spoon. Pass through a sieve and return to the pan.

Cook the gnocchi as above. Reheat the sauce and toss with the drained gnocchi, mix in the tomato, divide between plates.

Parsley Gnocchi with Chilli and Garlic

Chilli and garlic oil

---

2 garlic cloves	salt
1 teaspoon chilli, finely chopped	5fl oz/150ml extra virgin olive oil

---

Chop and crush the garlic. Place the chilli, garlic and salt in a small saucepan with the olive oil. Heat it until it feels hot when you dip your finger in it, then let it infuse for 10 minutes. Strain the oil and return it to the saucepan.

Parsley gnocchi

1lb 6oz/625g potatoes	salt, pepper
2oz/30g flat-leaf parsley	5oz/140g 'Farina 00'
(weight excluding stalks)	(see page 228)
2 egg yolks (size 2)	

To serve

Freshly grated Parmesan

Boil the potatoes in their skins. When they are cool enough to handle, skin them and pass them through a sieve or mouli-légumes. Bring a pan of salted water to the boil and cook the parsley for 4 minutes. Drain it and squeeze out as much water as possible. Using a large chopping knife, mince it.

Mix the egg yolks into the potato purée and season with salt and pepper. Stir in the parsley. Gradually work the flour into the potato. Do not mix more than is necessary – the dough will be sticky.

Prepare and cook the gnocchi according to the master recipe above. Rewarm the oil and dress them, and accompany with Parmesan.

See also:
Vichyssoise (page 20)
Chilled Wild Garlic, Potato and Saffron Soup (page 21)
Potato Gratin with Wild Mushrooms and Fontina (page 98)
Potato and Onion Tart with Horseradish Cream (page 149)

Pasta and Noodles

Dried Pasta

It was only when I came to write an article on pasta-making for *Vogue* that I became aware that there are some 400 or so varieties of pasta in existence. So great is the subject that a museum in Imperia, Italy, has been dedicated to it. The first recipes in this section rely on commercially produced dried pasta. These dried pastas should not be regarded as an inferior substitute for home-made fresh pastas; they are completely different. Both have their own qualities and characteristics which suit different preparations.

The names of pasta can be confusing. A millimetre of difference in the length or thickness gives rise to a different name, and there are also regional variations so that the same pasta may be called something different depending on the region. 'Shape' is also a lengthy subject: certain shapes suit certain sauces, and certain ways of preparation. Some types of pasta are designed to hold a sauce and others to let it run off. The bottom line in such sophistication must be the shape designed by Giugiaro, the automobile designer, for Voiello of Napoli. It is shaped as a squat wheel about 10 millimetres in diameter, with two tubes on either side; ridges inside the wheel are designed to hold the sauce, and once dressed it promises a succulent mouthful.

For myself, pasta pleasure derives from my own interpretation of what pastas suit what sauces. This offers any cook huge creative potential. Learning about pasta, both dried and fresh, should be a journey of exploration and discovery. I have given detailed instructions for making fresh pasta dough, rolling it, storing and cooking it (see page 228); once you have mastered these basics, enjoy that potential.

When cooking dried pasta, be sure to cook it in plenty of boiling water, about 2 pints/1.1 litres to 4oz/115g of pasta, 1 teaspoon of salt, and stir to separate it as soon as it is added. For broad strips of pasta such as pappardelle, add a shot of oil to the pan and add one strip at a time. Do not drain it too thoroughly, otherwise since it continues to absorb moisture it will take it from the sauce, leaving you with rather a dry dish. Dress the pasta immediately, and toss it with a little oil or butter if there is any delay.

There cannot be a cook in Britain who is not familiar with the phrase 'al dente': you should cease to cook most dried pastas while they still have a 'toothsome' quality. This involves standing to attention by the pan during the last minutes, testing it so as to catch it at just the right minute. Gino Santin advises, in his book *La Cucina Veneziana*: 'Trying to state an exact time for cooking pasta is a fairly thankless task. It all depends on the type of pasta (whether it's fresh and homemade, or dried), on the size of the pot, on the heat, and on the amount of water. As in all good cooking, you have to be there, and then you can take a strand out and taste it for the degree of doneness you like. Spaghetti and other dried pasta can be cooked until al dente – with a give to the tooth – but fresh pasta is too soft for that advice to hold true. Instead of watching the clock, you must watch the pot.' Fresh pasta can cook in as little as 1 minute.

Macaroni with Tomato

I have a soft spot for macaroni, at its best with a simple sauce such as this one, sweet and rich with the flavour of tomatoes, and some freshly grated Parmesan. While most types of pasta benefit from being left firm-to-the-bite, macaroni acquires a silky texture if you cook it a minute or two longer than you would other varieties.

Sauce

3lb/1.4kg marmande tomatoes	*3 garlic cloves, chopped*
sprig of thyme	*1 tablespoon tomato purée*
2 parsley stalks	*1 large basil leaf, shredded*
¹/₄ teaspoon fennel seeds	*pinch caster sugar*
2 tablespoons olive oil	*salt, pepper*

16oz/450g macaroni	*3oz/85g freshly grated Parmesan*

To make the sauce, cut a cone from the top of each tomato and slash a cross on the base. Skin them by plunging them into boiling water for 30 seconds, then into a basin of cold water. Remove the seeds and chop them. Contain the thyme, parsley stalks and fennel seeds in a piece of muslin.

Heat the olive oil in a saucepan, cook the garlic briefly until it releases its aroma, then add all the ingredients for the sauce to the pan, including the muslin sachet, and cook over a medium heat until it is thick and concentrated, about 30-40 minutes. Discard the muslin sachet and adjust the seasoning with sugar, salt and pepper.

Bring a large pan of salted water to the boil and cook the macaroni according to the instructions. Drain it and toss with the tomato sauce. Serve with a bowl of freshly grated Parmesan.

Penne with Cauliflower and Chilli

Any squat and tubular pasta can be used here. Both the cauliflower and the pasta should be on the firm side. The sauce is richly-flavoured and hot, and just coats the pasta and cauliflower. Parmesan would be out of place.

14oz/400g cauliflower florets
  (1 large cauliflower)
3 garlic cloves
2 level tablespoons tomato purée
1 teaspoon harissa

3 tablespoons extra virgin olive oil
1lb/450g tomatoes, peeled, seeded
  and chopped
salt, pepper
8oz/225g penne

Cut the cauliflower into ¹/₂ inch/1cm florets. Finely chop the garlic cloves. Dilute the tomato purée with 3 tablespoons of water and stir in the harissa. Take a deep frying pan or sauté pan and heat the olive oil. Cook the garlic until it gives off an aroma, then add the tomato solution, the tomato concassée and seasoning. Simmer the sauce for a couple of minutes. Add the cauliflower and cook, covered, for 7 minutes, stirring occasionally. It should remain on the firm side.

While the cauliflower is cooking, boil the pasta, leaving it firm to the bite. Drain it, though not too dry, and toss it with the cauliflower. Adjust the seasoning and serve.

Fettucini with Lemon

A book which has me sighing as I flick through it is *The Natural Cuisine of Georges Blanc*. No matter how radically my opinions change from year to year, it remains my all-time favourite cookery book, and this is one of the recipes in it. Part of M. Blanc's brilliance is that equal care and deliberation are applied to an extremely simple recipe such as this and to the more sophisticated ones. The original recipe calls for homemade fettucini, but dried will do just as well.

14oz/400g fettucini
grated zest of 4 well-washed
lemons
4fl oz/115ml white wine

5fl oz/150ml crème fraîche
3oz/85g Gruyère, grated
lemon juice
salt, pepper

Bring a large pan of salted water to the boil and cook the pasta, leaving it firm to the bite.

In a medium-sized saucepan, combine the lemon zest with the white wine and simmer for 3-4 minutes until it reduces by half. Drain the pasta and add to the pan, stir in the crème fraîche and Gruyère, and cook over a medium heat, tossing constantly, until the cream thickens slightly and the pasta is coated and very hot. Season to taste with lemon juice, salt and pepper, and serve.

Spaghetti with Pesto

While pesto is one of the best ways of coping with a glut of fresh basil, and can be kept, it is also at its best immediately it has been made. Spaghetti with pesto is such a simple classic, beautifully understated.

Traditionally Genoese pesto is made with basil, Parmesan cheese, pine nuts, olive oil and garlic. Once it was crushed in a pestle and mortar, releasing essences which would heighten its flavour. But I should imagine even the most conscientious Italian housewife makes full use of the food processor when time is tight. This traditional pesto is pungent, ringing with the flavour of basil. Used in small quantities it enhances soups, pasta, sauces and pizza. Do not be deterred from making it if Romano Pecorino is not forthcoming, use 2oz Parmesan in total.

Pesto

1oz/30g pine nuts	*1¹/₂oz/45g freshly grated*
1 garlic clove	*Parmesan*
salt	*¹/₂oz/15g freshly grated Romano*
3oz/85g basil leaves	*Pecorino*
8 tablespoons extra virgin olive oil	*pepper*

1lb/450g spaghetti	*salt, pepper*
extra virgin olive oil	

Heat the oven to 180°C/350°F/Gas 4 and toast the pine nuts for 5-6 minutes, until they are lightly golden. Chop and crush the garlic with a little salt, to a paste.

Make the pesto by placing the basil, pine nuts, olive oil and garlic in the food processor. Reduce it to a purée, incorporate the cheeses and season it. Cover and chill it. To store for a couple of weeks, seal the surface with a thin layer of olive oil.

Bring a large pan of salted water to the boil and cook the spaghetti according to instructions, leaving it firm to the bite. Drain it and toss with olive oil and seasoning. Mound into bowls and place a large spoon of pesto on top.

Asparagus Lasagne

Sheets of lasagne come flavoured with spinach or tomato. Many brands do not require boiling before they are layered and still produce excellent results. It is the 'no need to precook' variety that is required here.

The Fontina I find in Italian delicatessens melts to a gorgeous creamy consistency, but the one I find in supermarkets melts to a gooey rubber with rather an unpleasant 'nose' to it, likely to override the delicacy of this lasagne. If you are unable to find a decent Fontina you could choose another cheese with suitable melting properties.

Tomato sauce

1½lb/675g tomatoes	1 heaped teaspoon caster sugar
1 garlic clove	1 tablespoon tomato purée
1 tablespoon olive oil	salt, pepper

3lb/1.4kg asparagus	2½oz/70g freshly grated
12fl oz/325ml vegetable stock	Parmesan
3fl oz/85g white wine	salt, pepper
¾oz/20g unsalted butter	½lb/225g lasagne
½oz/15g plain flour	10oz/285g Fontina cheese, sliced
5fl oz/150ml crème fraîche	

First prepare the tomato sauce. Slice the tomatoes. Mince the clove of garlic, heat the olive oil in a saucepan and cook the garlic momentarily until it gives off its aroma. Add the tomatoes and remaining ingredients for the sauce and cook, covered, for 15 minutes. Remove the lid and cook until it reduces by a third.

Liquidize the contents and pass them through a sieve, adjust the seasoning, and reserve.

Cut the asparagus 1 inch/2cm towards the tip from where it becomes visibly tough. Finely slice the remaining green part from the tough ends before discarding them and reserve this. Peel the spears to within a couple of inches of the tip and cut into 2 inch/5cm lengths, cutting on the bias. Bring a large pan of salted water to the boil and cook the asparagus until it is quite tender. The length of time this takes will depend on the thickness of the spears. Drain, cool in cold water and reserve.

Bring the vegetable stock and white wine to the boil, add the finely sliced asparagus and cook covered for 10 minutes. Liquidize and pass through a sieve. Melt the butter in a small saucepan, add the flour and cook for a couple of minutes. Gradually incorporate the asparagus sauce and cook for several minutes, then stir in the crème fraîche and half the Parmesan. Adjust the seasoning.

Select a baking dish with sides 2-3 inches/5-8cm deep, about 8 x 12 inches/20 x 30cm, and coat the base with one third of the tomato sauce, reserving the remainder for the top of the lasagne. Next cover the base with a layer of lasagne, then some asparagus, and season this. Lay some slices of Fontina cheese over the asparagus, then spoon some asparagus sauce over. Continue to use up the ingredients so there are 3 layers of lasagne and 2 of the filling, ending with a layer of lasagne. Spread the remaining tomato sauce over and cover with foil. The lasagne can be prepared in advance to this point.

Heat the oven to 180°C/350°F/Gas 4 and cook the lasagne for 20 minutes. Remove the foil, scatter over the remaining Parmesan, and cook for a further 25 minutes until the top is patched with gold.

'Pad Thai'

No one who has trekked around Thailand can have done so without being sustained on numerous occasions by a large plate of 'Pad Thai'. I have fond memories of a small café in Bangkok, a wok stationed at the entrance and an old woman who spent most of her day standing beside it turning out 'Pad Thai' to order. She had been making it all her life and it was always wonderful, washed down by a glass of Thai beer. I still regret that this was before my days as a cook and I never asked for a lesson. A number of the ingredients must be bought from a specialist shop, but they all keep.

The actual cooking of the 'Pad Thai' takes only 3-4 minutes, so the art is to have all the necessary ingredients at the ready in separate bowls. If you are intending to have a good-sized plateful as a main course, this will feed only 2 people, but this quantity is as much as you should cook in one go in the wok.

3oz/85g sen lek noodles, or rice noodles
2 garlic cloves
1/2 teaspoon chilli, minced
4 spring onions
3 tablespoons light soy sauce
1 tablespoon lime juice
1/4 teaspoon chilli powder (or cayenne pepper)
1 level teaspoon caster sugar

2 tablespoons coriander leaves
2 tablespoons basil leaves
2 tablespoons arachide oil
1 egg (size 2)
4 1/2 oz/125g beansprouts
2 1/2 oz/70g cashew nuts, chopped
1 1/2 oz/45g preserved turnip, shredded
lemon quarters to serve

Cover the noodles with boiling water and soak for 5 minutes, drain and reserve. Finely chop the garlic cloves and reserve with the minced chilli. Trim the spring onions, shred them lengthwise and cut into 3 inch/8cm lengths.

Combine the soy sauce, lime juice, chilli powder and sugar. Leave the coriander leaves whole and make a chiffonade of the basil leaves.

Heat the arachide oil in a wok. Throw in the garlic and chilli and cook for a couple of seconds, add the spring onions, break in the egg and stir after a couple of seconds. Add the noodles, half the beansprouts, half the nuts and the preserved turnip and cook for a couple of minutes. Add the prepared sauce, then add the remaining nuts and beansprouts and after 1 minute pile on to a plate or plates. Scatter over the herbs and serve with lemon wedges.

Fresh Pasta

At its simplest fresh pasta consists solely of eggs and flour. Some people like to colour and flavour it, some to add oil, salt, or water. In Sicily it is made using white wine, and on a Sunday in the home a delicate pasta made only with flour and water is made, which must be cooked immediately. I am in favour of certain natural colourants and flavourings: wild mushrooms, truffles, saffron, and herb pasta all appeal, but like all innovation it is open to abuse and I have heard of some peculiar additions to dough.

Gino Santin has two restaurants in Belgravia, London: Santini's and L'Incontro. The food is Venetian, very elegant and more refined than the modern trend towards Italian food. A house speciality is the *'pasta mista'*, which gives you a taste of three or four different pastas and looks extremely pretty. When I ordered this, a plate arrived with a small pile of *'Pappardelle Santini'* – thick ribbons of pasta with an artichoke sauce; a few ravioli filled with spinach and ricotta and a sage butter drizzled over; a small pile of gnocchi with tomato and basil sauce; and some *'tagliatelle di funghi di bosco'* – tagliatelle with wild mushrooms. Gino Santin shies away from flavouring or colouring his dough and feels this is lost once the pasta is cooked and dressed. He relies on a basic dough for all his pastas, consisting simply of flour, eggs and mineral water. The flour used is a special Italian variety which can be found in an increasing number of delicatessens. The flour is graded 'Farina 00' and marked for pasta-making. It is soft and provides a good elasticity. The pasta can be thinly rolled yet retains some firmness when cooked. If you are unable to find this flour use ordinary plain flour instead.

The pasta at Santini's is coloured a remarkable saffron yellow, really quite bright. This is entirely due to the colour of the yolk. Gino Santin imports his eggs from Milan, and they have a bright orange yolk the like of which I have never seen in an English egg. I was so intrigued by these orange yolks that it sparked off a lengthy

hunt: talking to different farmers and producers to try and establish what can affect yolk colour. A free-range chicken will produce a yolk which is naturally darker than a battery-produced one, especially if it is maize-fed. But even these yolks did not compare to the Italian one. Musing over these findings with a friend one day, we thought it possible that the reason for the colour of the Italian yolks could be the concentration of sunlight in Italy and the way this affects the maize or grass on which the chicken feeds.

Until quite recently in Britain egg yolks were maintained at a desirable shade of yellow with the assistance of artificial dyes. Because this is now frowned upon, a half-way house has been reached so that dyes are still used together with the feed but they are called 'nature identical', and derive from natural products. If you make pasta with an egg that has been artificially dyed, the colour tends to come out in the cooking water. People often equate yolk colour with quality. If an egg has been produced naturally, then the yolk will be well-flavoured and the white will be firm and gelatinous. If the yolk has been coloured artificially, it will be no better than any other mass-produced egg likely to have an insipid-tasting yolk and a watery white. The point is to use good quality 'free-range' eggs. Unfortunately 'free-range' can vary in definition. Healthfood outlets are perhaps the most reliable suppliers of good eggs, as, dare I say it, are good butcher shops.

I have become very reliant on my Marcato 'Atlas' pasta-making machine. This is a small table-top machine which is clamped to the worksurface and rolls the pasta like an old-fashioned mangle. A variety of cutting attachments are available, though the thin and thick noodle cutters which come with the machine are sufficient. I prefer to cut ravioli and pappardelle by hand. Some small outlets which make pasta rely on an industrial machine which compresses the dough, forcing it out through nozzles. The dough is considerably drier than a hand-rolled pasta, and the machine also allows for the use of semolina. There is a small 'family' model of this machine, at

a price, but there is some debate about whether the pasta is as good as that produced by a hand-cranked machine.

Special trays are available for storing fresh pasta, with a wooden surround and a wire-mesh base. The air circulates around the pasta, preventing it from sticking. I tend to store the pasta on a floured plate in the fridge, covered with a tea towel, but I do not aim to keep it longer than a couple of hours. To talk about ways of storing fresh pasta for a long time is a contradiction in terms. Certainly good Italian restaurants will aim to make it freshly each day.

The vast majority of books recommend that pasta for noodles should be dried a little before it is cut. If you keep the dough on the dry side this may not be necessary. Only keep the pasta for a short while and flour the *sfoglia*, the rolled-out sheet of pasta dough, before you cut it. With practice you will come to recognize whether the dough needs to be dried a little before it is cut. If making noodles, loosely wind them into a nest and store them on a plate or in a floured tea towel. Store ravioli between floured parchment paper, cover with a tea towel and keep in the fridge. Many restaurants use the technique of blanching the pasta for 15 seconds then plunging it into cold water: noodles are tossed with a little oil and ravioli stored between oiled clingfilm. I generally use this method for ravioli.

Basic Pasta Dough

I was taught this method by Laura Santin, Gino Santin's daughter. The dough is slightly unusual because of the relatively low egg content and the addition of water. It is easier to handle than a dough made purely with egg and flour, and the resulting pasta is softer to eat. I have had consistent success with this method, which is the most important thing.

1lb/450g flour	*still mineral water*
3 eggs (size 2)	

Place the flour in a bowl, break in the eggs and mix with a fork. Bring the dough together, adding just enough mineral water for it to adhere. Keep it on the dry side, and if necessary add a touch more water when you start to knead. I find it easier to complete this last stage on a worksurface. Using the heel of your hand, knead the dough for 10 minutes until it becomes smoother in texture. Wrap it in clingfilm and rest it in the fridge for 30 minutes.

Divide the dough into 4, roll one piece at a time and keep the rest wrapped. Set the pasta rollers on the widest gauge, flatten the dough and start to feed it through the rollers. Do this about four times on the first setting, folding the sheet of dough in half each time and occasionally sprinkling it with flour. At this stage the rollers are kneading the dough. You need to put the dough through about 6 gauges, twice on some, folding it and flouring it as above. The *sfoglia* needs to be different thicknesses depending on what pasta will be made. For noodles, pappardelle and open ravioli, it is thin enough when the pink of your hand just starts to show through the dough. Sometimes the final gauge on the machine can roll the dough too thinly and a better result can be obtained by putting it through a wider gauge several times. The dough for ravioli should be rolled thinner than that for lasagne or noodles, since the edges will be double the thickness.

Pumpkin Ravioli with Sage Butter

Filling

2lb/900g pumpkin or
  1¹/₂lb/675g butternut squash,
  weight excluding skin and seeds
5oz/140g ricotta
1oz/30g freshly grated Parmesan

¹/₂ beaten egg (size 2)
a generous pinch of freshly grated
  nutmeg
salt, pepper

---

1 quantity of pasta dough
  (see above)

beaten egg

Sage Butter

5oz/140g good unsalted butter

10 sage leaves

To serve

black pepper
freshly grated Parmesan

Cut the pumpkin into cubes. Bring a large pan of salted water to
the boil and cook for 10 minutes. Drain, and when it is cool enough
to handle place in a tea towel and squeeze out as much water as
possible; be very thorough, as the filling must be dry. Place this
together with the other ingredients for the filling in the bowl of a
food processor and reduce to a smooth, thick paste. Season it well.

Roll the pasta as described on page 231. Cut into lengths about 16 inches/40cm long; the top sheet for the ravioli needs to be a little longer than the bottom sheet. Place teaspoons of the filling with 2 inches/5cm between them on one sheet. Brush the dough with beaten egg where the edges will join, and lay another sheet of rolled dough on top, taking care to ease any air bubbles out. Use a pastry cutter to cut the ravioli into squares about 3-4 inches/7-10cm and discard the trimmings. Continue with the remaining dough and filling and store as described above.

Prepare the sage butter by clarifying the butter as described on page 8. Infuse the warm butter with the sage leaves for 10 minutes and reheat when required.

To cook the ravioli, bring a large pan of water to the boil and cook for approximately 3 minutes. Divide the ravioli between the plates and spoon some sage butter over. Decorate with a sage leaf or two and a grinding of black pepper. Serve freshly grated Parmesan separately.

Ravioli with Fennel, Dolcelatte and Poppyseeds

This is a single circular ravioli, about 5 inches/12cm in diameter. It is filled with a julienne of fennel and chicory, sweated in a little butter, a slice or two of dolcelatte on top of this. It is poached for about 3 minutes, so that the cheese just melts, and is served with clarified butter and poppyseeds scattered over.

These ravioli need to be cooked as soon as they are made, which may not appeal to the cook who likes to have everything done in advance of a meal and then hang up his or her apron. But on occasions it is nice to make the preparation of a meal part of the party, especially if you have a large kitchen or it is part of the dining area. The extra chaos that making these ravioli might cause is small in comparison to the pleasure of eating them.

To make 6

pasta dough made with	*1oz/30g unsalted butter*
10¹/₂oz/300g flour, 2 eggs	*salt, pepper*
(size 2), still mineral water	*2¹/₂oz/70g dolcelatte*
8oz/225g fennel	*1 egg (size 2), beaten*
4oz/115g chicory	

To serve

5oz/140g unsalted butter, clarified
blue poppyseeds

Make the pasta dough according to the master recipe on page 230, wrap it in clingfilm and leave it to rest in the fridge. To prepare the filling, make a julienne of the fennel 2 inches/5cm long and blanch this in boiling, salted water for 1 minute. Drain and reserve.

Remove the outer leaf part of the chicory, reserve this for a salad, and make a julienne with the remainder. Melt the butter in a frying pan, add the fennel and the chicory, and sweat over a low heat for 8-10 minutes, seasoning it. Slice the dolcelatte into 6 thin slices.

Bring a large pan of salted water to the boil. To cook 6 ravioli at one time it is best to use two saucepans to avoid overcrowding them. To assemble the ravioli, roll the pasta as described on page 231. Flour the *sfoglia* and cut half into 6 inch/15cm lengths, and cut the other half for the top sheet of the ravioli about 1 inch/2cm larger. Place some of the fennel mixture in the middle of one of the smaller cut lengths, and place a slice of dolcelatte on top. Paint around this with the beaten egg, and place a larger piece of pasta on top, easing the air out of the ravioli. Using a fluted pastry cutter, trim to a circle about 5 inches/12cm in diameter. Prepare the rest of the ravioli in the same fashion, allowing one per person.

Reheat the clarified butter. Cook the ravioli in the boiling water for about 3 minutes, turning them once, and remove with a slotted spoon. Divide them between the plates, trickle over a little butter and scatter over some poppyseeds.

Ravioli 'all U'ovo' with Wild Mushrooms

As with the recipe above, this is a single circular ravioli. A version of this dish is served at Santini Milano in Milan: inside the ravioli is an egg yolk, a couple of slices of Fontina cheese and shavings of white truffle. It is cooked just long enough for the outside of the egg yolk to set and the Fontina to melt. The result as you cut into it and the egg yolk runs out can be imagined. If you keep truffle oil to hand, then flavour the clarified butter to be drizzled over at the end.

To make 6

---

pasta dough made with	*salt, pepper*
10¹/₂oz/300g flour, 2 eggs	*3oz/85g Fontina cheese*
(size 2), still mineral water	*6 egg yolks (size 2)*
8oz/225g wild mushrooms	*1 egg (size 2), beaten*
³/₄oz/20g unsalted butter	

To serve

5oz/140g unsalted butter, clarified
freshly grated Parmesan

Make the pasta dough according to the master recipe on page 230, wrap it in clingfilm and leave it to rest in the fridge. Pick over the wild mushrooms and slice or tear them if large, heat the butter in a frying pan and cook them for several minutes until soft, season them and reserve. Slice the Fontina cheese.

If making 6 ravioli bring two large pans of salted water to the boil. Roll the pasta as described on page 231. Flour the *sfoglia* and cut half into 6 inch/15cm lengths, and the other half which will be used for the top sheet of ravioli about 1 inch/2cm larger. Take one of the smaller pieces of pasta and place some mushrooms on it, making a well in the centre for the egg yolk. Separate the egg and discard the white – the yolk must remain whole. Drop this in the centre of the mushrooms, season and place a couple of slices of Fontina on top. Brush with the beaten egg around the edge of the ravioli where the edges will join. Place a larger sheet of pasta on top, easing the air out. Using a fluted pastry cutter, cut a ravioli about 5 inches/12cm in diameter. Continue this process with the rest of the pasta and filling.

Reheat the clarified butter. Cook the ravioli in the boiling water for about 3 minutes, turning them once. Remove with a slotted spoon and divide between the plates. Trickle over some clarified butter and serve with the Parmesan.

Saffron Tagliatelle with Broad Beans and Mangetouts

This is a very simple fresh pasta dish. The flavours are delicate, and the tagliatelle is wonderfully silky when it is coated with crème fraîche. To achieve a really yellow pasta you have to cheat a little: use a combination of saffron filaments and powder, one to give the flavour and the other the colour. Cut the basil at the last minute.

For the pasta dough

---

20 saffron filaments and 1/8 teaspoon powdered saffron or 1 standard sachet	10 1/2oz/300g flour 2 eggs (size 2) still mineral water

---

3lb/1.4kg fresh broad beans, to yield 1lb/450g podded beans (frozen can be used) 8oz/225g mangetouts 4 heaped tablespoons crème fraîche	lemon juice salt, pepper 2 tablespoons chives, coarsely cut 2 tablespoons basil, cut into strips

---

First make the pasta dough. Toast the saffron filaments in a dry frying pan for 1 minute, grind them in a pestle and mortar, and infuse them together with the powdered saffron in 1 tablespoon of boiling water for 10 minutes. Proceed to make pasta dough according to the master recipe (page 230), using the saffron tincture to bind the dough (a little more water than this may be needed). Rest the dough for 30 minutes in the fridge wrapped in clingfilm.

Shell the broad beans if they are fresh. Bring a pan of salted water to the boil and cook them for 6 minutes, then plunge them into cold water. If they are large, remove the outer pale husk. If you are using frozen broad beans, cover them with boiling water to defrost them, then remove the pale husks. Remove the tops from the mangetouts and blanch them in boiling water for 1 minute, then plunge them into cold water and reserve.

Roll the pasta according to the instructions on page 231 and cut the *sfoglia* into 12 inches/30cm lengths. Flour these and cut into tagliatelle. Coil loosely around your fingers and store as suggested on page 230.

Bring a large pan of salted water to the boil. Heat the crème fraîche in a saucepan and season with lemon juice, salt and pepper. Add the broad beans and mangetouts to heat through, but do not cook more than is necessary. Cook the pasta for approximately 2 minutes. Drain and toss with the sauce, add the herbs and adjust seasoning.

Warm Salad of Pappardelle with Herbs and Baby Spinach

I have never been a fan of pasta salads – as pasta cools it alters in texture from something luxuriant and silky to something stodgy and firm. This dish, however, is an exception – the pappardelle is tossed with some herbs and baby spinach leaves while it is hot, and the salad is served warm. Make sure that the herb leaves are young and tender, and likewise the baby spinach.

pasta dough made with
  10¹/₂oz/300g flour, 2 eggs
  (size 2), still mineral water

Dressing

1 dessertspoon red wine vinegar
salt, pepper

4 tablespoons extra virgin olive oil
4 tablespoons arachide oil

Salad

2oz/55g baby spinach
2 level tablespoons chives, snipped
  1 inch/2cm long
1 level dessertspoon tarragon leaves

1 level dessertspoon basil, torn
1 level tablespoon flat-leaf parsley
  leaves

To make the pappardelle, prepare and roll the pasta as described on page 231; cut it into strips 1 x 5 inches/2 x 10cm, using a pastry cutter. Flour these and stack them. Cover with a tea towel and keep in the fridge for up to a couple of hours.

To make the dressing, whisk the vinegar with the seasoning. Add the oils. Add a shot of oil to a large pan of boiling water and cook the pasta for 1-2 minutes, separating the strips before they go into the pan. Drain the pasta and toss with the dressing, adding all the leaves and herbs at the last minute. Adjust the seasoning and serve immediately.

Rice and Polenta

Risottos

A risotto is perfectly cooked when you judge it to be so, not when you have used all the stock. The amount of liquid quoted is an upper limit. Since the stock is kept simmering on the stove for half an hour while the risotto is cooking, it will evaporate during the process, making it difficult to give an exact quantity to use.

Wild Mushroom Risotto

Make this risotto with any mixture of dried and fresh wild mushrooms: recently I cooked it using dried trompettes des morts and porcini, and fresh girolles, Paris mushrooms and chestnut mushrooms. In fact, the dried wild mushrooms impart such character to the risotto that you could make it with fairly ordinary cultivated mushrooms and still get excellent results.

This risotto is extremely filling, so precede or follow it with something relatively light.

1oz/30g dried wild mushrooms
12oz/340g fresh wild mushrooms
3oz/85g unsalted butter
1³/4-2 pints/1-1.1 litres vegetable stock (including mushroom liquor)
1 small onion

10oz/285g arborio rice
5fl oz/150ml white wine
2oz/55g freshly grated Parmesan
salt, pepper
flat-leaf parsley and chervil, finely chopped

Cover the dried wild mushrooms with plenty of boiling water, about ½ pint/300ml, and leave them to soak for 15 minutes. Wipe the fresh mushrooms and slice them. Melt ½oz/15g of butter in a frying pan and cook half the mushrooms for 3 minutes. Cook the other half in the same way and reserve in a bowl.

Drain the soaked mushrooms, strain the liquor if it seems gritty, and make up to 2 pints/1.1 litres with the stock; keep this simmering on the stove while the risotto cooks. Coarsely chop the soaked mushrooms and add them to the fresh ones.

Finely chop the onion. Heat 1½oz/45g of the butter in a heavy-bottomed pan and sweat the onion over a low heat until it is translucent and soft. Add the rice and cook for 1-2 minutes. Add the wine and when it has been absorbed, add the mushrooms to the pan and start to pour in ladles of the simmering stock, one or two at a time – at no stage should the rice be flooded. The risotto will take about 20-25 minutes to cook. Remove from the heat while it is a touch too moist and the grains are still firm; it will have absorbed the excess liquid by the time it arrives on the table.

Stir in the Parmesan and the remaining butter. Adjust the seasoning and serve it with a succinct sprinkling of chopped parsley and chervil.

Asparagus Risotto with a Pea Sauce

There is a fortuitous overlap in the season of fresh peas and asparagus, albeit a brief one. Should the longest day of the year greet you with a provocative downpour, foil its belligerence by immersing yourself in the comfort of this dish. There is no denying that perfectly cooked fresh asparagus eaten with butter and brown bread is hard to beat, but a risotto allows hidden qualities of flavour to emerge and a well-made dish of it is memorable.

Prepare a vegetable stock with onion, leek, celery, carrot, the ends of the asparagus and some of the pea pods. Discard the very end of the asparagus stalk, where the presence of mould spores will taint the stock. Coarsely chop the vegetables and sweat them in butter for 10 minutes, cover them with water, and add some seasoning. Simmer the stock for 30 minutes and strain it.

Sauce

2lb/900g fresh peas	15fl oz/450ml vegetable stock
2 shallots	pinch caster sugar and salt
1oz/30g unsalted butter	2 dessertspoons crème fraîche

Risotto

1¹/₂lb/675g finger-thick asparagus	10oz/285g arborio rice
2 pints/1.1 litres vegetable stock	5fl oz/150ml white wine
1 small onion	2oz/55g freshly grated Parmesan
2¹/₂oz/70g unsalted butter	salt, pepper
	finely chopped flat-leaf parsley

To make the sauce, shell the peas, reserving the pods. Finely chop the shallots, melt the butter in a saucepan and sweat them for a minute or two. Add the peas, about 6 of the pods with stalks removed, the stock and the sugar and salt. Bring this to the boil and cook it covered for 10 minutes. Purée the sauce, pass it through a sieve, stir in the crème fraîche, and adjust the salt.

Trim the asparagus stalks where they become clearly fibrous and inedible, reserving the trimmings for the stock. Peel the stalk from this end to the point where it becomes green and tender, about 3 inches/8cm from the tip. Cut the spears into 2½ inch/6cm lengths, cutting on the bias. If the spears are very thick, halve them lengthwise.

Bring the vegetable stock to the boil, add the asparagus, bring the stock back to the boil and simmer for 4 minutes. Remove the asparagus to a bowl and keep the stock simmering on the stove.

Finely chop the onion. Heat 2oz/55g of the butter in a heavy-bottomed pan and sweat the onion over a low heat until it is translucent and soft; it should not colour. Add the rice and cook this for 1-2 minutes. Pour in the wine and allow the rice to absorb it. Start to add the simmering stock a ladle at a time – at no stage should the rice be flooded. Add the asparagus after the first couple of ladles of stock have been absorbed. Remove from the heat while the risotto is a touch too moist and the rice is still just firm, and it should then arrive on the table the correct consistency.

Reheat the sauce. Stir the Parmesan and the remaining butter into the risotto. Adjust the seasoning and serve it with some parsley scattered over and a ribbon of sauce around the outside.

Nettle Risotto

It was with great scepticism that I donned armour, equipped myself with scissors, a basket and protective gloves and went nettle-topping. The idea of eating a substance that one has come to know in a different context, flowers, or in this instance nettles, seems to require a shift in acceptance of the substance. Stinging nettles suffer doubly from this dilemma – most of us have painful childhood memories of searching out a dock-leaf to relieve a smarting calf. In any event, having gathered a basketful of potentially injurious fronds, and cooked my first risotto, I was instantly hooked. The texture is excellent, the flavour rich and strong. Nettles have a high iron content and a surprising 5.5 per cent of protein.

Nettles can be picked from March to June. Take the tender top of the plant, the first few centimetres. After June the leaves develop minute crystalline particles in the leaves which can make eating them unpleasant. It is important to wash nettles well; the minute hairs covering them collect dirt and dust, and for this reason it is advisable to pick them away from the road-side.

10oz/285g nettle-tops
1 small onion
3 tablespoons extra virgin olive oil
2 garlic cloves
9oz/250g arborio rice
5fl oz/150ml white wine

1½ pints/900ml vegetable stock
salt, pepper
1oz/30g unsalted butter
1½oz/45g freshly grated
    Parmesan, ½oz/15g finely
    shaved Parmesan

Wearing rubber gloves pick over the nettles, then wash and dry them thoroughly. Chop the onion, heat the olive oil in a large saucepan and cook the onion and whole garlic cloves until soft and translucent. Discard the garlic cloves. Add the nettles and toss until they have wilted. Add the rice and cook for a couple of minutes. Add the white wine, and as soon as it is absorbed start to add the simmering stock in ladles, just covering the nettles and rice, but not swamping it. Season the risotto. When the rice appears to be just cooked, but on the firm side, after about 20 minutes, remove it from the heat and stir in the butter and grated Parmesan cheese; adjust the seasoning. Serve the risotto with the fine shavings of cheese scattered over.

Paella with Rouille

Hardware stores in Spain stock a variety of paella pans, ranging in size from 10 inches/25cm to a metre in diameter. These are shallow iron pans with a handle on either side, the principle being that the rice should be thinly layered over the base and receive an even cooking. Stores also sell special outdoor burners on tripods, which will accommodate the larger pans. Many gas ovens in Spain are equipped with a specially designed wide-jet gas ring for preparing the 'national' dish. A large saucepan can be used in lieu of a *paellera*.

Paella is the sister of the Italian risotto, and though it traditionally includes a range of ingredients taboo to the vegetarian, a perfectly delicious version can be made without them. As with a risotto, the flavouring ingredients are cooked along with the rice so the flavours are absorbed, but water is added in one go at the beginning rather than gradually throughout the cooking. The finished paella is drier than a risotto. When it is cooked in a traditional pan it is often covered with a cloth and left for 10 minutes while the rice absorbs any additional moisture, then the grains separate more effectively when plumped up with a fork. Though the dish is not traditionally served with rouille, it works a treat, particularly since in this version you do lose some of the flavour usually contributed by the fish or meat. With Italian vegetarian risottos this is not such a problem, since they can be bolstered by a generous addition of Parmesan at the end.

People took umbrage when frozen peas replaced fresh ones in British gastronomy a few decades ago. Personally I like frozen petits pois, and see them as a different variety of vegetable altogether. There are instances when frozen ones can be more appropriate than fresh. Such is the case here, and at the risk of heresy I recommend you use tiny, sweet, frozen peas.

25 saffron filaments
1 garlic clove
2 shallots
3oz/85g okra
6oz/170g courgette
1 orange/red pepper
2 artichokes, and juice of 1 or 2
    lemons to prevent discoloration
4oz/115g asparagus sprue
1 stick celery

2oz/55g fennel
3 tablespoons extra virgin olive oil
10oz/285g arborio rice
5fl oz/150ml white wine
salt, pepper
22fl oz/650ml vegetable stock
4oz/115g frozen petit pois
2 heaped tablespoons flat-leaf
    parsley, finely chopped

To serve

lemon wedges

Toast the saffron in a dry frying pan for 1 minute, then grind in a pestle and mortar and infuse with a little boiling water for 10 minutes.

Prepare the vegetables. Mince the garlic and shallots and reserve them. Trim the stalk of the okra and slice the courgette. Core and deseed the pepper and cut it into strips. Pare the artichokes (page 6), removing the chokes, cut them into wedges, and reserve in lemon juice. Cut the asparagus stalk at the point where it becomes fibrous and discard it. Slice the celery and fennel.

Heat the olive oil in a heavy-bottomed saucepan or *paellera*. Add the garlic and shallot and cook for a minute or two, then add the prepared vegetables and cook them for a couple of minutes. Add the rice and cook a further 2 minutes, then pour in the wine, add the saffron tincture, season with salt and pepper, and when the wine is absorbed add the stock. Bring this to the boil and cook at a steady simmer, adding the peas 5 minutes before the end. It will take about 20 minutes. You can cover the pan and leave it for 5-10 minutes to absorb additional moisture, then plump up the rice. Adjust the seasoning and stir in the parsley. Accompany with the rouille and lemon wedges.

Rouille

The use of harissa in the rouille gives it a hot and sharp bite: the brainchild of Rick Stein, proprietor of the Seafood Restaurant in Padstow, Cornwall.

1oz/30g *day-old bread*	2 egg yolks (size 2)
1 *red pepper, roasted, skinned and seeded*	9fl oz/250ml *extra virgin olive oil*
	7fl oz/200ml *arachide oil*
5 *garlic cloves*	*lemon juice*
2 *heaped teaspoons harissa*	*salt*

Place the bread, pepper, garlic and harissa in a food processor and reduce to a paste. Add the egg yolks, then trickle in the oils in a thin stream as though making a mayonnaise. Season with lemon juice and salt.

Wild Rice Salad with Baby Corn, Coriander and Almonds

Garlic shoots are a newcomer to supermarket shelves, and welcome. In appearance they are like a fat chive, not dissimilar to wild garlic in flavour, and they are milder than the familiar cloves of garlic. They can be preferable to raw cloves in salads, for instance, and are useful added to sautéed potatoes or other such dishes when you want the presence of garlic without being overwhelmed.

Wild rice is nutty by nature, so this salad is quite robust to eat and decidedly healthy and nutritious. It is also colourful and flavoured with the favoured combination of fresh coriander, ginger, garlic and almonds.

Dressing

1 dessertspoon lemon juice	3 dessertspoons extra virgin
1 dessertspoon lime juice	olive oil
salt, pepper	6 dessertspoons arachide oil
1 heaped teaspoon ginger root, finely diced	

3oz/85g wild rice	salt, pepper
4oz/115g white rice	3 spring onions
2 heaped tablespoons flaked almonds	3 garlic shoots or 1 garlic clove
3oz/85g fennel	2 heaped tablespoons coriander leaves
3oz/85g sugar snaps	1oz/30g little red Treviso chicory
3oz/85g baby corn	leaves, or radicchio torn into
extra virgin olive oil	pieces, white removed

First prepare the dressing: whisk the lemon juice and lime juice with salt and pepper, add the ginger, and if using a garlic clove instead of garlic shoots, crush and add this also. Add the oils.

Boil the wild rice in salted water for 45 minutes. Strain into a sieve and run cold water through it. Place in a bowl. Simultaneously prepare the white rice in the same fashion, cooking it for 15 minutes, and combine with the wild rice. Toast the almonds in the oven for 7 minutes at 180°C/350°F/Gas 4 until they are lightly golden.

Cut the fennel into ¼ inch/0.5cm dice, remove the tails from the sugar snaps and blanch these two vegetables for 1 minute, then plunge into cold water. Halve the corn lengthwise, brush with olive oil, season and char-grill, or cook in a dry frying pan. Allow to cool. Finely slice the spring onions and garlic shoots, and mix these together with the prepared vegetables into the rice.

Just before serving, strain the dressing and toss this with the salad, mix in the almonds, coriander leaves and Treviso and adjust the seasoning. Eat straight away.

Polenta

It is possible to buy both fine and coarse polenta, and I have got into the habit of using the coarse ground variety, but the difference is not so great should you fall upon the fine ground type. Polenta can be made to any thickness, and it firms on cooling, so the thicker polentas can be grilled or fried. I like to char-grill polenta, rather than pan-fry it or grill it under a conventional grill, partly because of the flavour this imparts, but also because you achieve a more delicate crispness. Polenta is like a blank canvas: it can act as the base to a hundred dishes, it can be cooked in a variety of ways and flavoured with numerous ingredients. I like polenta, but I would not choose to swap it for pasta or potatoes and sometimes I feel its popularity is overrated. The two recipes which follow are my preferred ways of cooking it: one firm and char-grilled, flavoured with Parmesan, with slowly baked leeks and olives and a spoonful of mascarpone on top; the other a soft and creamy polenta, with lots of pan-fried mushrooms and their juices on top to seep into the polenta, served with a rich Fontina cream.

Once upon a time polenta took time and constant attention to prepare. A pan of water was brought to the boil and the polenta was poured like sand into the water, stirring all the time to prevent lumps forming. It was cooked for about 45 minutes, then turned out on to a wooden board. Thankfully modern 'quick cook' varieties have evolved, which may still take 20-40 minutes to acquire their desired texture and degree of doneness but suffer a little more neglect than the old-fashioned type and do not require constant stirring. It is also considerably easier and less likely to result in lumps if the polenta is heated along with the water, rather than pouring it into already boiling water. Although a thick crust forms on the base of the pan, a good soak and it will lift off with ease.

Leeks Braised with Olives served with Char-grilled Polenta and Mascarpone

1¾lb/800g leeks
2½oz/70g black olives
5 sprigs thyme
8fl oz/225ml white wine
1½oz/45g unsalted butter
salt, pepper

1¾ pints/1 litre water
9oz/250g coarse-grain polenta
1 heaped teaspoon salt
1½oz/45g freshly grated
  Parmesan
extra virgin olive oil for grilling

To serve

5oz/140g mascarpone

First prepare the leeks, which require a long slow cooking. Trim and remove the dark green shoots and the outer layer, halve them if they are long, and wash them well. Bring a large pan of salted water to the boil and cook the leeks for 5 minutes. Cool them in cold water, then halve them lengthwise. Pit and halve the olives, and arrange the leeks cut surface up in a casserole, layering them with the olives and the thyme sprigs. Pour over the white wine, dot with the butter and season. Cover closely with paper parchment and then the lid. Bake for 1¼ hours at 160°C/325°F/Gas 2. Discard the thyme sprigs when cooked. The leeks can be cooked in advance and reheated if wished.

Place the water, polenta and salt in a medium-sized saucepan and bring to the boil, stirring. Cook for about 20 minutes over a low heat, stirring occasionally. Initially, the polenta behaves like a mud spring and spits and plops, so half cover the pan with a lid. When it is cooked, stir in the Parmesan and pour into a shallow container so it has a depth of around ¾ inch/1.5cm. Cover the surface with clingfilm and allow to cool. Cut into triangles to give 2 per person.

To serve, heat the griddle, brush the polenta with the oil and grill until it is charred, about 10 minutes each side. Pour the liquid from the leeks into a small saucepan and reduce until it amalgamates and thickens slightly. Divide the polenta between plates, spread some mascarpone on to it and place some leeks on top, and spoon the sauce over.

Soft Polenta with Mixed Mushrooms and Fontina

This recipe is imported from the mountains surrounding Trento in Northern Italy. After a hard morning's hiking in the hills we stopped at a *malga*, a very basic and rustic café with a milking shed attached. The menu gave little choice: standard fare is a large wedge of yellow polenta, a mass of wild mushrooms gathered in the surrounding woods, smoky and resinous, and a bowl of melted cheese – the locals know this as 'mountain cheese', and it is made with the milk from their own cows.

8oz/225g coarse-grain polenta	*salt, pepper*
2 pints/1.1 litres water	*1¹/₂lb/675g mixed mushrooms*
1 heaped teaspoon salt	*2oz/55g unsalted butter, clarified*
6oz/170g Fontina cheese	*1 garlic clove, peeled and minced*
6fl oz/175ml double cream	*1 heaped dessertspoon flat-leaf*
1 tablespoon white wine	*parsley, finely chopped*

The polenta will take 30 minutes to cook. Place the polenta, water and salt together in a saucepan, bring to the boil, stirring, then let it splutter gently for 30 minutes until thick, just stirring occasionally. You can half cover the saucepan with a lid to stop it spitting.

Make the sauce at the same time as cooking the mushrooms: slice the Fontina, heat it with the cream and wine in a saucepan and season it.

Scrape the dirt from the mushrooms and tear them into pieces, or slice them. Heat a little of the clarified butter in a frying pan and when it is smoking hot throw in some mushrooms, covering the base of the pan, and cook for 2-3 minutes, adding a pinch of garlic just before the end. Reserve the mushrooms and cook the remainder in the same fashion. Stir in the parsley and season.

Serve a large dollop of polenta with the mushrooms on top and some Fontina sauce poured over.

Chocolate, Fruit Tarts
and Other Puddings

Chocolate

There is no doubt that the face of chocolate is changing. The path to connoisseurship, though, is a long and complicated one, and the issue of 'real chocolate' has been fraught with confusion. In their haste to persuade people to start eating real chocolate, some have suggested that the higher the percentage of cocoa solids a dark chocolate contains, the better it is likely to be. While there is some truth in this, it is akin to saying that an alcohol that is 15 per cent proof is a better quality than one which is 11 per cent proof. Cocoa, like grapes or coffee beans, will differ in quality depending on its origin, its type and how it has been grown. Just as important is how it is handled once harvested. Unfortunately, the only information you are likely to find on a wrapper will be in terms of percentage; 55-75 per cent cocoa solids is a good indicator, but do not be conned, more does not necessarily mean better.

The other point to be clarified is the difference between chocolate and 'couverture', which has nothing to do with cocoa percentage. Couverture chocolate, by definition, is one which contains more than 31 per cent cocoa butter. Cocoa butter is an expensive ingredient usually substituted with undisclosed fats in cheaper chocolate candy. It is the magical ingredient that gives chocolate its crack, its shine and its melt-in-the-mouth quality, being solid at 33°C and molten at 34°C. Chocolatiers use it because it provides a fluidity when melted which allows for greater control when coating a centre. For the home cook, couverture lends a beautiful silky texture to *'petits pots au chocolat'*, chocolate sauces, and truffles, but it is not suitable for very light or aerated confections because of its high fat content.

Other features of good chocolate are real rather than artificial vanilla, and a low sugar content. Sugar is used by large manufacturers to disguise the poor quality of cocoa beans. Chocolatier Christian Constant believes that 'sugar is to chocolate what salt is to other food', and it should be used to bring out the flavour of the cocoa.

The French company Valhrona is the leading brand name in the field of pure chocolates; dark couvertures are their speciality. By careful selecting and processing Valhrona have created a sophisticated range of chocolates with different end flavours, including a range of intensely flavoured '*grands crus*' made from beans from a restricted area. They also produce a high quality dark chocolate especially for baking purposes. These chocolates are becoming more widely available, and I would not be surprised to see large commercial producers following suit with their own high quality dark chocolate or couverture following Valhrona's success – let's hope.

TO MELT CHOCOLATE

Chop the chocolate small, and place it in a bowl over some hot but not boiling water. Less heat than you imagine is required to melt chocolate, especially couverture. Do not rush it; periodically remove the bowl from the heat and let the added warmth continue to melt the chocolate – even once it is melted it should not feel warm to the touch. Keep in mind that chocolate burns at a low temperature, and water is an enemy, so keep all utensils dry.

Churros y Chocos

In Seville, come Semana Santa, Feria, New Year or for that matter any Saturday night when the tired habitués of the flamenco bars spill out on to the streets at dawn, Sevillians will make for the nearest bar or stall selling 'churros y chocos'.

'Churros y chocos' are the original 'dunkin' donuts'. *Churros*, made simply from flour and water, are piped through a fluted nozzle; they can be shaped as a horseshoe, or more festively as a large curled length cooked in a giant cauldron of oil, and broken up once cooked. They are eaten with hot chocolate, dipped into it as they are eaten. At breakfast the chocolate is usually a rich drink, but at times it resembles a thin sauce, as in this version, intended as a dessert. It is wickedly rich and defies every guideline on cholesterol. Certainly as a national breakfast it belies the slender and graceful forms of most Sevillians – perhaps they work it off in the flamenco bars.

A *churrera* is a specially designed instrument for piping the dough, but a piping bag with a star-shaped nozzle ½ inch/1cm in diameter can be used. The *churros* can be piped in advance and stored between layers of parchment paper or clingfilm for several hours. Pipe the dough into 4 inch/10cm lengths or equivalent shapes.

Chocolate sauce

10fl oz/275ml milk	¼oz/7g caster sugar
2 inch/5cm stick cinnamon	5oz/140g bitter chocolate or dark
1 vanilla pod, slit	couverture, coarsely chopped
1 heaped teaspoon cocoa, sifted	2 egg yolks (size 2)

Bring the milk to the boil with the cinnamon stick and vanilla pod; infuse for 15 minutes. Strain the milk and return it to a saucepan; boil with the cocoa and sugar for 1 minute. Add the chocolate to the milk and melt. Whisk to a smooth liquid. Blend a little of the chocolate with the egg yolks and strain back into the pan. Reheat the sauce over a low heat until it thickens. It can be reheated but should never boil.

Churros

This recipe comes from *The Festive Food of Spain* by Nicholas Butcher.

18fl oz/500ml water	*¹/₂ teaspoon salt*
9¹/₂oz/275g plain flour	*a tasteless oil for deep-frying*

Boil the water, add the sifted flour and salt and work to a smooth, thick paste. Cook for a couple of minutes. Remove and cool, then pipe it (see above).

Deep-fry the *churros* in oil until golden and crisp. Drain on kitchen paper. Serve immediately with the hot chocolate sauce.

Chocolate Mousse

9oz/250g *bitter chocolate*	1 *tablespoon dark rum or brandy*
5 *egg yolks (size 2)*	6 *egg whites (size 2)*

Melt the chocolate in a double boiler. Incorporate the egg yolks and then the alcohol. Whisk the egg whites until they are stiff. Mix a couple of spoons of this into the chocolate mixture and then the rest as lightly as possible. Pour into a bowl or individual bowls and chill for several hours.

Petits Pots au Chocolat

I have it on the authority of someone who eats chocolate mousse daily that this is even better. These chocolate creams should be made with couverture chocolate; they take full advantage of the 'liquid silk' nature of a couverture. They are small and delectable and it is quite normal for a diner to go for a second.

8fl oz/225ml double cream
6fl oz/175ml whole milk
4 egg yolks (size 2), whisked
3oz/85ml milk couverture chocolate

5oz/140g dark couverture chocolate
1 dessertspoon Tia Maria

Bring the cream and milk to the boil and pour on to the egg yolks – it should thicken to a thin custard instantly. Pass through a sieve, cover the surface with clingfilm, and cool to room temperature. Melt the chocolate, blend half the custard with the chocolate, and then the rest, and stir in the Tia Maria. Spoon into little coffee cups, cover with clingfilm and chill.

Chocolate Mousse Tart

Pastry

4oz/115g plain flour	*2oz/55g unsalted butter*
1¹/₂oz/45g caster sugar	*1 egg yolk (size 5)*

5oz/140g dark couverture chocolate	*1 dessertspoon caster sugar*
3 egg yolks (size 2)	*4 egg whites (size 2)*

First prepare the pastry by reducing the flour, sugar and butter to crumbs in a food processor. Add the egg yolk, and a little water if necessary, to bring the dough together. Roll thinly and line a shallow 8 inch/22cm tart tin (there should be pastry left over). Chill for 30 minutes.

Preheat the oven to 180°C/350°F/Gas 4, line the pastry case with foil and baking beans, and bake for 15 minutes. Remove the foil and bake for another 10 minutes until lightly golden and crisp. Turn the oven up to 200°C/400°F/Gas 6.

Melt the couverture, whisk the egg yolks and caster sugar until pale, and incorporate the chocolate. Whisk the egg whites until stiff, fold one third into the chocolate mixture, then the rest. Pour into the pastry case and bake for 7 minutes. Serve when it has cooled to room temperature.

Pear Tart with Quince and Pine Nuts

While the original marmalade was in fact quince jam, quinces have all but disappeared in this country and can now be found only in a few specialized shops and in people's gardens. They are a popular fruit in Spain: *crema de membrillo* is a sweetened quince paste widely available there which often accompanies cheese. It is possible to find it over here also, and it imparts its musky fragrance to this tart when thinly spread over the base of the pastry case. The paste can also be made from fresh quinces should you chance upon them, but there is no denying the intensity of the task; 'very much a family enterprise', as Jane Grigson puts it. She details how to prepare such a paste in *Jane Grigson's Fruit Book*, a book no cook should be without (nor, for that matter, should they be without her *Vegetable Book*).

If you are serving this as a dessert, accompany it with cream, crème anglaise or ice cream.

Pastry

6oz/170g plain flour	*3oz/85g unsalted butter*
2oz/55g caster sugar	*1 egg yolk (size 2)*

Filling

4oz/115g unsalted butter	*7oz/200g sweetened quince paste*
3oz/85g caster sugar	*14oz/400g firm but ripe pears*
2 eggs (size 5)	*3 tablespoons pine nuts*
4oz/115g ground almonds	*icing sugar*
1 tablespoon Poire William	
liqueur	

To make the pastry place the flour, sugar and butter together in the bowl of a food processor and reduce them to crumbs. Add the egg yolk and enough cold water to bring the dough together. Butter and flour a 9 inch/22cm tart tin with sides 1½ inches/4cm deep, and press the dough into it. Chill this for 1 hour.

Line the pastry case with foil and baking beans and bake for 15-20 minutes at 180°C/350°F/Gas 4 until it has set and just started to colour; it will receive a second baking, so it should not be completely cooked. Remove the foil and beans and turn the oven down to 170°C/325°F/Gas 3.

Cream together the butter and sugar for the filling. Separate the eggs and reserve the whites. Add the egg yolks to the butter and sugar and then the ground almonds. Incorporate the Poire William liqueur.

Shop-bought varieties of quince paste usually come in firm blocks, so work it with a spoon until it is spreadable, and spread it thinly over the base of the pastry case. Peel and core the pears, slice them and arrange evenly over the base.

Whisk the egg whites until stiff and lightly fold into the creamed mixture; spoon over the fruit. Scatter the pine nuts on the surface of the tart and bake it for 25-35 minutes. When it has cooled dust it with icing sugar.

Tarte Tatin with a Vanilla 'Crème Anglaise'

Stephanie and Caroline Tatin cannot have known just how appreciated their mistaken discovery of the *'tarte renversée'* would be, as Caroline Tatin accidentally piled apples cooked in butter and sugar into a pastryless tin, then rectified it by placing a circle of pastry on top, and gave birth to one of France's best loved desserts. Whether or not this story is true, it is a fitting legend for such a magnificent tart. It is also delicious served with a Calvados sabayon, made according to the recipe on page 279, using Calvados instead of kirsch.

The apples are about 2 inches/5cm deep, with just a thin base of pastry.

First the base of the mould is coated with caramel, and halves of apple are arranged spherical-side down in the dish, which ensures a beauteous surface of golden domes when it is turned out. While this bakes in the oven the remainder of the apples are cooked with butter and sugar in a frying pan, then pressed on top of the domed apples, a circle of puff pastry is fitted and the whole thing baked and then inverted.

6oz/170g caster sugar	*1 tablespoon Calvados*
4oz/115g unsalted butter	*6oz/170g puff pastry*
11 Golden Delicious apples	

Place 3 oz/85g of the caster sugar with 2 tablespoons of water in a small saucepan and cook to a golden caramel. Off the heat, add 1¹/₂oz/45g butter cut into small cubes. Coat the base of a deep 8 inch/20cm round-based mould with the caramel – I use the base of a pyrex casserole for this.

Preheat the oven to 180°C/350°F/Gas 4. Peel the apples, halve 4 of them and remove the core. Lay these halves curved side down

in the mould so they overlap slightly, placing one in the centre. Cover this with foil and bake it for 25 minutes.

Quarter and core the rest of the apples. Melt the remaining butter in a frying pan and add the remaining sugar. Cook for a minute or two until they amalgamate, then add the apples and cook for 20 minutes, adding the Calvados half-way through. Adjust the heat as necessary to ensure the sauce dries out; the resulting apples should be coated in a thick, light golden syrup.

Pour these on top of the apples in the mould, pressing them down firmly to achieve a flat surface. Roll the pastry $^1/_8$ inch/0.25cm thick and cut to fit the surface of the apples, allowing $^1/_2$ inch/1cm for shrinkage. Lay this loosely over the apples and bake for 30 minutes in the preheated oven. Let the tart stand for 45 minutes before inverting it on to a plate. Serve it with the vanilla crème anglaise.

Vanilla Crème Anglaise

---

1 pint/600ml milk	*7 egg yolks (size 2)*
1 vanilla pod	*3oz/85g caster sugar*

Pour the milk into a saucepan. Slit the vanilla pod and scrape the seeds into the milk. Bring this to the boil with the pod and infuse for 15 minutes. Remove and discard the pod.

Whisk the egg yolks and sugar together until they are pale. Blend a little of the milk with the egg yolks and return this to the saucepan. Cook the custard over a low heat, stirring it until it thickens and coats the back of a spoon, though it must not boil. Strain through a sieve into a jug. Cover the surface with clingfilm and refrigerate it once cool.

Apple Tart with a Whisky Sauce

This is a very simple apple tart. The base is like a shortbread and as it cooks it soaks up the butter, sugar and apple juice, becoming beautifully rich. The apples are thinly sliced and fanned out on the pastry, and the tart is glazed once it is cooked.

Pastry

3oz/85g unsalted butter	*1¹/₂oz/45g plain flour*
4¹/₂oz/125g ground almonds	*2oz/55g icing sugar*

5 Granny Smith's apples	*caster sugar*
1oz/30g unsalted butter	*2oz/55g sieved apricot jam*

Butter and flour a 12 x 9 inch/30 x 22cm Swiss roll tin. Place all the ingredients for the pastry in the bowl of a food processor and bring together into a ball. Line the base of the prepared tin by pressing the dough into it, without making sides to the tart case, sprinkling with flour if it is sticky. Rest for 30 minutes in the fridge. Preheat the oven to 180°C/350°F/Gas 4, prick the base of the case with a fork and bake for 10 minutes until beginning to colour.

Turn the oven to 200°C/400°F/Gas 6. Peel, halve and core the apples. Slice thinly into crescents, discarding the end slices, then fan these out lengthwise and place in rows on the pastry. Dot with butter, sprinkle with sugar and bake for 20 minutes, watching the outside of the pastry to make sure it does not burn. Warm the apricot jam until it thins, then glaze the tart using a pastry brush. Serve warm, but not straight from the oven.

Whisky Sauce

15fl oz/450ml milk	*5fl oz/150ml double cream*
7 egg yolks (size 2)	*3 tablespoons whisky*
3oz/85g caster sugar	

Bring the milk to the boil. Whisk the egg yolks with the sugar, pour some of the milk over, and blend until smooth. Return the egg mixture to the pan and cook the custard until it thickens without it boiling. Strain, place in a bowl, cover with clingfilm and cool.

Whip the cream, whisk into the custard and stir in the whisky.

Pecan Pie

Serve this warm with some ice cream, or with the whisky sauce above. Either golden syrup or corn syrup, available from some healthfood shops, can be used.

Pastry

5oz/140g plain flour	*3oz/85g unsalted butter*
2oz/55g caster sugar	*1 egg yolk (size 2)*
pinch salt	

7oz/200g pecan kernels	*9oz/250g syrup (see above)*
3oz/85g unsalted butter	*1/2 teaspoon vanilla extract*
5oz/140g demerara sugar	*2 heaped tablespoons plain flour*
4 eggs (size 2)	*1/4 teaspoon salt*
2 tablespoons dark rum	

Prepare the pastry by placing the flour, sugar, salt and butter in a food processor, and reducing it to crumbs. Add the egg yolk and sufficient water to bring the dough together. Wrap it in clingfilm and chill it for 30 minutes.

Preheat the oven to 180°C/350°F/Gas 4. Roll the pastry thinly and line a 9 inch/22cm tart case, 1½ inches/4cm deep, with a removable base; there should be about a third remaining. Line with foil and baking beans and bake it for 20 minutes, then remove the foil and baking beans and cook a further 5 minutes until lightly golden. Toast a third of the pecans, whole, for 8 minutes in the oven and chop the remainder.

Turn the oven down to 165°C/325°F/Gas 3. Cream together the butter and demerara sugar. Add the eggs, then the rum, syrup and vanilla. Incorporate the flour and salt. Mix the chopped pecans into the mixture. Pour this into the tart case, set the toasted whole pecans on the surface, and bake for 40 minutes.

Almond Crumble with Cape Gooseberries and Raspberries, with a Kirsch Sabayon

This crumble is quite delectable, with or without its cloak of sabayon. Obviously the combination of fruits can be altered to suit the larder; try to include some berries, but counter them with a blander fruit such as apple or pear.

If the fruit is very ripe, sprinkle it with sugar and leave it in a bowl for 30 minutes to exude some of its juices; these can be added to the sauce. A certain amount of juice is desirable, but the finished product should not look like an island of crumble surrounded by a quagmire.

2oz/55g flaked almonds	*2oz/55g oats*
8oz/225g raspberries	*2oz/55g plain flour*
caster sugar	*4oz/115g ground almonds*
8oz/225g Cape gooseberries	*4oz/115g soft brown sugar*
3 eating apples	*6oz/170g unsalted butter*
1 tablespoon kirsch or other	
* eau-de-vie*	

Preheat the oven to 180°C/350°F/Gas 4 and toast the flaked almonds for 8 minutes until they are lightly golden. If the raspberries are very ripe, sprinkle them with caster sugar and set them aside for 30 minutes; if any juice is given out, reserve it to add to the sauce. Remove the Cape gooseberries from their husks. Peel, halve and core the apples and slice them. Arrange the fruit in a suitable baking dish. Sprinkle over a couple of dessertspoons of caster sugar and trickle over the kirsch.

Combine the oats, flour, ground almonds and brown sugar in the bowl of a food processor. The butter must be well chilled – cut it

into pieces, combine with the dry ingredients and give it a burst at high speed until it forms a crumble. Care must be taken to stop the motor as soon as a crumble is formed, otherwise the mixture will wrap itself into a neat ball of biscuit dough.

Mix the flaked almonds into the crumble and scatter it over the fruit. Bake the pudding for 45 minutes at 170°C/325°F/Gas 3 (check it after 20 minutes to see that it is not colouring too quickly, and turn the oven down if it is). The crumble can be served at any temperature. I like it about 25 minutes after it comes out of the oven; cooked fruit never tastes good boiling hot.

Kirsch Sabayon

Use an eau-de-vie which will complement the fruit in the crumble. Coat a pear and blackberry crumble with a sabayon made with Poire William liqueur, for instance.

4 egg yolks (size 2)	*3 tablespoons kirsch*
1³/₄oz/50g caster sugar	*4 tablespoons water*

Set the lower half of a double boiler over a gentle heat with ¹/₂ inch/1cm of water in it. Whisk together the egg yolks and sugar in the top half of the double boiler and place this over the bottom half. Heat the egg yolks for a couple of minutes, whisking them. Add the kirsch and water a little at a time, whisking continuously until it is thick and forms soft mounds.

Remove it immediately from the heat and spoon it over the crumble, or decant to a jug and serve straight away.

Orange Savarin with Rum

Traditionally a savarin is made in a circular mould with a hole in the centre and a rounded base; the centre can be filled with custard, cream or fruit. I prefer to make it in an 8 inch/20cm cake tin and simply slit and fill it.

In this recipe the cake, which is light and spongy, is soaked with a rum and orange flavoured syrup, and filled with an orange custard which has been baked in the oven.

There are various methods of preparing the basic dough. This version comes from Elizabeth David's *English Bread and Yeast Cookery*. The savarin mixture always remains a batter, and it is beaten rather than kneaded. The whole operation is a great deal easier and quicker than making a brioche; and considering the temperament of many yeasted cakes and breads, it is more or less foolproof.

Orange Custard

5fl oz/150ml double cream	5 eggs (size 2)
4fl oz/115ml orange juice and zest of the oranges used (approx. 2)	5oz/140g caster sugar

---

Savarin

8oz/225g strong white flour	4fl oz/115ml milk
1 level teaspoon salt	3 eggs (size 2), beaten
2 teaspoons caster sugar	3oz/85g unsalted butter
1/4oz/7g yeast or equivalent dry	

Orange and Rum Syrup

7fl oz/200ml fresh orange juice	*6 tablespoons dark rum*
6oz/170g caster sugar	

The orange custard needs to be prepared several hours in advance of the savarin. To prepare this, heat the cream to boiling point and infuse it with the orange zest for 15 minutes. Whisk the eggs and sugar together, then stir in the orange juice and the cream. Pour this into a baking dish so it is a couple of inches deep, cover it with foil and cook it for 1½ hours at 125°C/225°F/Gas ½. Liquidize it to a smooth cream, cover and chill it.

To make the savarin, sieve the flour and salt into a bowl, add the sugar and, if you are using dried yeast, add it now too. If using fresh yeast, warm the milk to blood temperature, cream it with the sugar and yeast and let it stand for 10 minutes until frothy. Add this and the beaten eggs to the flour and mix to a lumpy batter. Cover it with a cloth or plastic bag and leave it to prove in a warm place (21°C/70°F) for 45 minutes. The batter should have doubled in volume and be spongy and light.

Melt and cool the butter and beat it into the batter, continuing to beat for 5 minutes. Butter and flour an 8 inch/20cm cake tin and pour the batter into it. Cover it and leave it to prove for 40 minutes or so until it has almost doubled in volume.

To prepare the syrup, sieve the orange juice and place with the sugar in a small saucepan. Heat this to 116°C/240°F on a jam thermometer, then remove from the heat and stir in the rum.

Heat the oven to 190°C/375°F/Gas 5 and cook the savarin for 25 minutes. Leave it to cool for a few minutes in the tin, then remove and slit it and pour equal quantities of the syrup over the cut surfaces. When it is cool fill the centre with the whipped orange custard. Keep this chilled.

Toffee Pudding

This recipe is adapted from one in *The Constance Spry Cookery Book*. It is homely, unfussed, very quick and quite divine. It is very sweet, and there is little I can offer by way of countering this, other than to add more cream.

---

3 heaped tablespoons sultanas
sweet wine
4oz/115g unsalted butter
1oz/30g demerara sugar

8oz/225g golden syrup
5oz/140g white bread
* (weight excluding crusts)*
milk

Place the sultanas in a small saucepan, just cover them with sweet wine and cook over a low heat until they absorb the wine and plump up; reserve these. Place the butter, sugar and golden syrup in a small saucepan and cook until it reaches 120°C/250°F on a jam thermometer.

Cut the bread into fingers, dip each one briefly into the milk so that they are wet but not sodden, and place them in a serving dish. Scatter over the sultanas, pour over the sauce, and toss the bread fingers so they are coated. Eat immediately with plenty of cream.

Sticky Toffee Pudding

I am not sure why this should be 'sticky toffee pudding' and the above simply 'toffee pudding' when in truth they are both as sticky as each other. This is more like a 'steamed pudding', in fact it is a basic cake mixture with sultanas which is baked in a bain-marie in the oven, the outside coated with a rich butterscotch. Serve with crème anglaise (see page 273) or double cream.

Caramel

4oz/115g caster sugar	1³/4 oz/50g unsalted butter
juice of ¹/2 orange	3 tablespoons double cream

4oz/115g sultanas	¹/2 teaspoon orange zest, finely grated
¹/4 teaspoon bicarbonate of soda	
2¹/2oz/70g unsalted butter	2 eggs (size 5)
4oz/115g caster sugar	6oz/170g plain flour, sieved
¹/2 teaspoon vanilla extract	1 teaspoon baking powder, sieved

First place the sugar and orange juice in a small saucepan and make a caramel. Off the heat whisk in the butter in small pieces, and stir in the cream. Pour into a 1¹/2 pint/900ml pudding basin and chill until hard. Soak the sultanas in ¹/2 pint/300ml of boiling water with the bicarbonate of soda for 10 minutes.

Heat the oven to 180°C/350°F/Gas 4. Cream together the butter and sugar, then add the vanilla and zest. Incorporate the eggs, flour and baking powder, then fold in the fruit. Spoon on top of the caramel, place a round of buttered parchment on the surface, cover the top with foil and tie this to the rim. Bake for 1 hour 15 minutes in a bain-marie, so the water comes two-thirds of the way up the sides. Unmould the pudding on to a plate and serve in wedges.

Tocino del Cielo with Oranges

Tocino del cielo is a type of rich, thick crème caramel. Of Spanish origin, it translates to the unlikely title of 'heavenly bacon', or 'sky bacon' on some menus in Spain. This recipe comes from *The Flavours of Andalucia* by Elisabeth Luard. She says it found its name when a nun omitted the egg whites from a sweet she was making; the result, she said, was only fit for pigs. The oranges cut through the sweetness and marry well with the caramel.

Caramel

3oz/85g caster sugar	juice of 1/2 lemon
2 teaspoons water	

Custard

12oz/340g caster sugar	1/2 pint/300ml water
2 inch/5cm strip of lemon peel	12 egg yolks (size 2)

Oranges

8 large oranges	Cointreau
1 1/2 oz/45g caster sugar	

Preheat the oven to 180°C/350°F/Gas 4. Place the ingredients for the caramel in a saucepan and cook to a dark, golden syrup. Coat the base of a 7 inch/18cm baking tin, either square or round. Keep the tin to one side.

Simultaneously prepare the custard by placing the sugar, lemon peel and water in a saucepan and heating them to 114°C/240°F (use a jam thermometer to measure this, it may read 'soft ball'); this will take about 20 minutes. Remove and discard the lemon peel. Whisk the yolks at a high speed in a food processor, then slowly dribble in the syrup whisking continuously. Pour the custard on top of the caramel, which will have hardened somewhat so the custard will settle on the top rather than mixing with it. Cover the surface of the custard with a round of greaseproof paper.

Place a shallow bain-marie in the oven, with ¹/₂ inch/1cm of boiling water in it, place the *tocino del cielo* in this and cook for 30 minutes; it should be firm. Once it is cool, remove the paper and cover with clingfilm. Refrigerate until serving.

Zest and juice 4 of the oranges, and place together with the sugar in a saucepan. Reduce to a third of the original volume and strain. Once it is cool, add Cointreau to taste.

Remove the skin and pith from the remaining oranges, and by running a thin-bladed knife between each segment extract the orange segments. Place these in a bowl with the syrup. Cover and chill until required.

To serve the *tocino del cielo* cut it into squares or wedges and remove using a palette knife, placing the pieces caramel-side up on each plate. The *tocino* will be lightly coated with the caramel but most of it remains on the base of the tin. Serve with the oranges. Cream is not necessary and would be inappropriate.

Cinnamon Blancmange with Poached Apples and Honey Biscuits

³/₄ sachet of gelatine, or 0.3oz/5g
  (or vegetarian substitute)
3 inch/7.5cm stick of cinnamon
1 pint/600ml double cream

3oz/85g vanilla sugar
¹/₂oz/15g caster sugar
6 egg yolks (size 2)

Sprinkle the gelatine on to a little boiling water and leave it to dissolve. Break up the cinnamon in a pestle and mortar. Heat the cream with the cinnamon to boiling point. Whisk together the sugars and egg yolks. Pour some of the cream on to the egg mixture and return it to the pan. Stir it over a low heat until it thickens, without boiling it. Blend a ladle of this with the gelatine, then stir this back into the custard.

Liquidize the custard and strain it through a fine-mesh sieve. Pour into a bowl or ramekins. Cover with clingfilm and chill once it is cool.

Poached Apples

¹/₂ pint/300ml apple juice
¹/₂ pint/300ml sweet wine
³/₄oz/20g caster sugar

6 cloves
6 eating apples
1 tablespoon Calvados

Place the apple juice, sweet wine, sugar and cloves in a saucepan and bring to the boil. Peel, halve and core the apples. Poach these in the liquor for 10 minutes, covering the pan. Remove them to a bowl using a slotted spoon, reduce the juice to 4fl oz/115ml, strain it over the apples and stir in the Calvados. Once it is cool, cover and chill until required.

Honey Biscuits

As one seven-year-old friend of mine put it: 'I think these would be nice dipped into wine, mummy.'

8oz/225g unsalted butter	*1 teaspoon baking powder*
6oz/170g caster sugar	*1 teaspoon bicarbonate of soda*
12oz/340g plain flour	*3 tablespoons clear honey*

Cream together the butter and sugar in a food processor until they are pale. Sift the dry ingredients and incorporate them. Add the honey. Cover and chill the dough for several hours or overnight.

Preheat the oven to 150°C/300°F/Gas 2. Form the dough into balls the size of a walnut, rolling them between your palms. Space them 2 inches/5cm apart on baking sheets and bake for 17 minutes or until they are a deep gold. Leave them on the trays to firm up for around 5 minutes, then remove them to a rack to cool.

To serve the dessert, unmould the cinnamon blancmange by running a knife around the edge of the mould and inverting it. Serve it in slices, or as individual ones, accompanied by the poached apples and honey biscuits.

Lovage Syllabub with Madeleines

This is one of the most unusual desserts I know. I have tried it out on many people, who have also taken instantly to the flavour. Lovage is a decorative herb to have in your herbaceous border. Cut it back to a stump each autumn and by June the following year it will probably be the tallest bush in the border. Use only the young shoots. This syllabub is also a good voice for mint, and a way of exploring the various mints and their flavours. It is very pungent, almost vulgarly so, and typically Edwardian.

---

juice of 1 lemon
1 heaped teaspoon finely grated
lemon zest
2oz/55g caster sugar

7fl oz/200ml double cream
3fl oz/85ml sweet wine
³/₄oz/20g lovage

Place the lemon juice, the zest and the sugar in a bowl and leave for at least 2 hours. Stir to dissolve the sugar, though it may not dissolve completely. Whip the cream until it just starts to hold its shape, then add the wine in about 3 lots, whisking between each addition. There is a danger of the mixture splitting if the wine is added too quickly. Finally add the lemon and sugar mixture and whisk until it is thick and fluffy.

Chop the lovage, fold into the syllabub, and leave for at least half an hour. Though the syllabub will keep well in the fridge for 24 hours, it may require a 'rewhisk' if some of the liquid separates out. Serve it with madeleines hot from the oven.

Madeleines

(makes 12-14 large madeleines)

Traditionally madeleines are baked in a special tray giving small scallop-shaped cakes, fluted on the underside. They can be tiny, and served as petits fours, partially dipped into chocolate, or larger, eaten as they have barely cooled. These cakes are light and meltingly soft, perfect for tea, to accompany desserts, or mid-morning.

2 eggs (size 2)	pinch of salt
2¹/₂oz/70g caster sugar	1 level teaspoon baking powder
1oz/30g vanilla sugar	2oz/55g ground almonds
finely grated zest of 1 lemon	4oz/115g unsalted butter, melted
2oz/55g plain flour	icing sugar to dust

Whisk the eggs and both sugars together until they are pale, then add the lemon zest. Sift the flour, salt, and baking powder, and fold these and the ground almonds into the egg mixture, but take care not to overwork. Likewise mix in the melted butter.

Rest the mixture in a cool place for 30 minutes. Preheat the oven to 190°C/375°F/Gas 5. Brush the insides of the cake moulds with melted butter. Spoon the mixture into the prepared moulds, filling each one two-thirds full. Bake them for 10 minutes. Run a knife around the perimeter and turn them out on to a rack to cool. When barely cool, dust with icing sugar and eat straight away.

Crème Brulée

Layering the caramel surface is Marco Pierre White's idea. Accompany with a separate fruit dish if you want to tone down its richness; personally I am happy to wallow in it.

---

6 egg yolks (size 2)	1 vanilla pod
3 heaped tablespoons caster sugar	1 pint/600ml double cream

Caramel

demerara sugar

Preheat the oven to 140°C/275°F/Gas 1. Whisk the egg yolks and pass them through a sieve, then whisk them with the sugar. Slit the vanilla pod and scrape the seeds from the centre, blending them with the egg yolks and sugar. Stir in the cream. Pour into a dish to a depth of 1-1½ inches/2-4cm and place in a bain-marie in the oven for 1 hour until it has set.

Grind some sugar in an electric grinder and sieve a fine film over the surface of the custard. Possibly the most effective way to caramelize the sugar is to take a blow-torch to it, on a lowish flame so as not to scorch the sugar. If such theatre seems daunting, then take your chances with a hot grill, though it can be hard to get an even melting; watch the sugar intently as it melts to a golden caramel to make sure that it does not burn. Repeat this with another film of sugar and, if you think it needs it, a third. The result should not be too chunky, just a very delicate, thin layer of crisp caramel. Cover the dessert and chill it in the fridge for a couple of hours.

Bibliography

Bareham, Lyndsey, *In Praise of the Potato*, Michael Joseph, 1989
Beck, Simone, Bertholle, Louisette & Child, Julia, *Mastering the Art of French Cooking, Volumes 1 & 2*, Penguin, 1987
Bhumichitr, Vatcharin, *Thai Vegetarian Cooking*, Pavilion, 1991
Blanc, Georges, *The Natural Cuisine of Georges Blanc*, Macmillan, 1988
Blanc, Raymond, *Cooking for Friends*, Headline, 1991
Butcher, Nicholas, *The Festive Food of Spain*, Cathie, 1991
David, Elizabeth, *English Bread and Yeast Cookery*, Penguin, 1987
Del Conte, Anna, *The Gastronomy of Italy*, Bantam Press, 1987
Del Conte, Anne, *Secrets from an Italian Kitchen*, Bantam Press, 1989
Domingo, Xavier, *The Taste of Spain*, Flammarion, 1992
Esquire Party Book, Arthur Baker Ltd, 1935
Graham, Peter, *Classic Cheese Cookery*, Penguin, 1988
Gray, Patience, *Honey from a Weed*, Prospect Books, 1986
Grigson, Jane, *English Food*, Penguin, 1986
Grigson, Jane, *Jane Grigson's Fruit Book*, Michael Joseph, 1991
Grigson, Jane, *Jane Grigson's Vegetable Book*, Michael Joseph, 1991
Hazan, Marcella, *The Classic Italian Cookbook*, Macmillan, 1980
Hazan, Marcella, *The Second Classic Italian Cookbook*, Macmillan, 1990
Jaffrey, Madhur, *A Taste of India*, Pan Books, 1987
Luard, Elisabeth, *The Flavours of Andalucia*, Collins & Brown, 1991
Madison, Deborah, *The Greens Cookbook*, Bantam Press, 1987
Ortiz, Elizabeth Lambert, *The Encyclopaedia of Herbs, Spices and Flavourings*, Dorling Kindersley, 1992
Phillips, Roger, *Wild Food*, Pan, 1983
Roden, Claudia, *A New Book of Middle Eastern Food*, Penguin, 1986
Romer, Elizabeth, *Italian Pizza and Savoury Breads*, Michael O'Mara, 1987
Round, Jeremy, *The Independent Cook*, Barrie & Jenkins, 1985
Roux, Michel and Roux, Albert, *Patisserie*, Macdonald, 1986
Santin, Gino, *La Cucina Veneziana*, Ebury Press, 1988
Savoy, Guy, with Langlois, Guy, *Vegetable Magic*, Ebury Press, 1986
Schneider, Elizabeth, *Uncommon Fruits and Vegetables*, Harper and Row, 1986
Spry, Constance & Hume, Rosemary, *The Constance Spry Cookery Book*, Dent, 1978
Toklas, Alice B., *The Alice B. Toklas Cookbook*, Brilliance Books, 1983
Waters, Alice, Curzon, Patricia & Labro, Martine, *Chez Panisse Pasta, Pizza and Calzone*, Random House, 1984
Wells, Patricia, *Bistro Cooking*, Kyle Cathie, 1990
Wolfert, Paula, *Good Food from Morocco*, J. Murray, 1990
Yan-Kit's *Classic Chinese Cookbook*, Dorling Kindersley, 1987

Index